THE
LAST
LINK

An Unbreakable Formula for
Eliminating Hidden Profit Killers

THE LAST LINK

Closing the Gap That Is Sabotaging Your Business

GREGG CRAWFORD

GREENLEAF
BOOK GROUP PRESS
www.gbgpress.com

Published by Greenleaf Book Group Press
4425 S. Mo Pac Expy., Suite 600, Austin, TX 78735

Distributed by Greenleaf Book Group LP

For ordering information or special discounts for bulk purchases, please contact
Greenleaf Book Group LP at 4425 S. Mo Pac Expy., Suite 600, Austin, TX 78735
(512) 891-6100.

Design and composition by Greenleaf Book Group LP
Cover design by Greenleaf Book Group LP

Publisher's Cataloging in Publication Data:

Crawford, Gregg.
    The last link : closing the gap that is sabotaging your
business / Gregg Crawford. -- 1st ed.
        p. : ill. ; cm.
    Includes index.

    ISBN-13: 978-1-929774-42-5
    ISBN-10: 1-929774-42-7

1. Sales management. 2. Customer relations. 3. Business
planning. 4. Success in business. I. Title.

HF5438.4 C73 2007
658.81   2006937703

Printed in the United States of America on acid-free paper

07 08 09 10 11 12   10 9 8 7 6 5 4 3 2 1

First Edition

CONTENTS

ACKNOWLEDGMENTS

Over the past twenty-five years my firm, BayGroup International, and I have worked to provide solutions for some of the greatest companies in the world. Our journey together has generated the experience, refinement of process, and lessons in executing strategy that form this book. The motivation for this book is to give back to the clients, the institutions of higher learning (including the Stanford University Graduate School of Business, the Stanford University Law School, and the University of California Hastings Law School), the business associates, and the friends who have helped shape the paradigms and practices that my colleagues and I have formulated and executed all over the world for a quarter of a century.

I want to thank Ben Crawford, Jay Cohen, Ron D'Andrea, David Mears, and Bob Rehfeld, in addition to the many Fortune 500 clients (some included below) that my firm and I have worked closely with over the past twenty-five years. Our work together helped form the ideology found in this book.

Agilent Technologies	Microsoft
American Express	NEC
AT&T	Owens Corning
Autodesk	Rockwell Automation
BEA Systems	S.C. Johnson & Son
BellSouth	Scottish Widows
Cisco Systems	Sodexho
Dell Inc.	Solectron
Hershey Foods Corporation	T-Mobile USA
Linear Technology	United Parcel Service

This book would not have been possible without two very special colleagues who made major contributions throughout its development—Deborah Nikkel and Paul Hennessey. Both Deborah and Paul spent countless hours helping to shape the words that you are about to read. Specifically, Paul's contributions to model and content development and Deborah's collaborative and creative writing and editing skills are evident throughout the book. In addition, I would like to thank the Greenleaf Book Group team for their guidance and encouragement in bringing *The Last Link* to the marketplace.

Finally, I would like to thank my wife, Katherine, and our children, Benjamin and Whitney, for their love and support over the years as BayGroup International and the content for this book evolved.

SECTION 1
INTRODUCTION

1

THE BROKEN LINK

If you want to make your numbers,
you need to execute strategy at the point of customer contact.

You can innovate, strategize, optimize, and systematize, but at the end of the day, it always comes down to one thing, doesn't it?

Are you making your numbers?

It's the measure of success in business. Period. The bottom line is always the same. Did we make our projections? Are we growing market share? Is revenue where it should be? Are our margins strong and improving? Is the business on a steady and predictable growth trajectory?

When the numbers are right, Wall Street, investors, and the media support everything you're doing. You're a hero when a successful merger takes place, a master when you introduce a new product line that gives your company distinct market advantage. You're a magician when you carve out a whole new market segment. You're a mystic when you divest the company of obsolete business units before they falter and bring the overall company value down.

But as soon as one success has passed, the pressure to achieve the next set of goals, to meet the next set of numbers, is on. It's the nature of the market. Financiers want to invest only in companies that show predictable, reliable performance. Analysts are increasingly reluctant to endorse the stocks of companies that are not growing revenue and margins—and even of those that are. If they aren't growing it at a rate that meets or surpasses market growth, it doesn't count.

Not meeting your numbers undermines your prestige in the market-place and can do irreparable harm to your competitive standing. That's not new. What is new is the rapid growth of challenges that make it difficult to make your numbers:

- More than ever, buyers are saying, "We perceive product parity and price disparity between you and your competition." This can drive price and profits down.

- In many industries, the rate of new competitor entry into the market is increasing, and new lower-priced alternatives threaten formerly secure profit margins.

- Customer demands and faster service response and shorter product life cycles are increasing the pressure to sell, contract, and deliver solutions faster than ever before. This makes it more likely that the profitability of each sale will be lessened and that costs of delivery will be excessive.

- Professional buyers preoccupied with reducing costs are now the rule rather than the exception. Highly trained and rewarded on their ability to negotiate lower prices, these newly empowered purchasing professionals make it harder than ever to establish and charge for the true value of a company's solutions. At the same time, more and more buying decisions are being made by risk-averse committees prone to making incremental rather than large-scale buying commitments.

- In an ever more global economy, there is increased pressure to drive and deliver global contracts that must compete in terms of price with companies located in countries with low labor and resource costs.

These threats to profitability can no longer be met through cost cutting alone, which for most organizations has reached the point of diminishing returns as a method of enhancing profit. This leaves the future to those who can

- Help customers see the value of their solutions, creating expanded sales opportunities with expedited sales cycles that close more profitably
- Create an "insurance policy" for unexpected disruptions in the business environment by deploying an effective strategy execution plan
- Ensure sustained, predictable sales and earnings growth

In *The Last Link*, you will learn how to consistently achieve all of these goals. The answer lies in executing strategy at the point of customer contact.

WHY STRATEGY FAILS

Corporate strategy plots out a company's best shot to succeed, and organizations spend enormous amounts of time, money, and effort designing strategies. They need to if they want to compete in today's business environment under ever-increasing pressure from shareholders and financial analysts to continually improve company profitability, cash flow, and share price. A solid strategy that focuses the entire organization on a critical set of financial goals can mean the difference between failure and success.

So companies develop sales and marketing strategies to meet the new threats to profitability on a corporate, regional, and account level. They spend immense amounts of time and money on computer systems, management consultants, initiatives, and training to document, track, and refine those strategies with the hope that the strategies will be the key to making the numbers.

But all of this activity doesn't mean their strategies will succeed or their companies will meet expectations. Even well-established businesses frequently underperform, as evidenced by the snapshot presented in figure 1-1 that shows how the stock price of several notable companies fared when compared against the industry average performance between August

FIGURE 1-1   *The "underperforming" companies listed below all have market values greater than $10 billion, and they all missed the mean quarterly estimates of Wall Street analysts for at least two of the four quarters between August 2004 and August 2005.*

Company Name	Net Sales ($ in millions)	Industry Group	Under-performance (against industry average)
Waste Management	$12,809	Environmental control	– 2.8%
General Mills	$11,244	Food	– 5.9%
International Paper	$26,245	Forest products and paper	– 20.8%
Morgan Stanley	$43,760	Diversified financial services	– 20.8%
General Motors	$190,675	Auto manufacturers	– 24.0%
Lucent Technologies	$9,412	Telecommunications	– 30.6%
Anheuser-Busch	$15,029	Beverages	– 31.2%
JPMorgan Chase	$71,824	Diversified financial services	– 36.0%
Maxim Integrated	$1,672	Semiconductors	– 40.9%
Marsh & McLennan	$12,124	Insurance	– 54.6%
Merck & Co.	$22,116	Pharmaceuticals	– 60.3%

2004 and August 2005. None of these companies lack the ability to analyze the situation, understand their problems, or make strategic investments to solve them. So why did they fail to meet their goals?

When you think of the way a business runs, you might think of a chain—each individual link performing its duty, all pulled in the same direction by the same force. Each link represents a particular function of the organization. The corporate strategy is the force that aligns all the links and pulls them in the right direction, unified and working together to achieve common goals. Every link has a vital purpose and fulfills it, making sure the chain remains strong.

But a strong, fully functional chain isn't the reality of most organizations. Why? Because strategy fails.

"Ninety percent of corporate strategies fail," say Robert Kaplan and David Norton, authors of *The Balanced Scorecard: Translating Strategy into Action*.[1] And according to Bain & Company, "All companies must grow to survive, but only 1 in 5 corporate growth strategies succeeds."[2] Often, the financial failures of a company are laid at the feet of poor strategy formulation, but that is not the conclusion the research supports.

So why *do* strategies fail? Because although companies put huge effort into designing, discussing, and launching their strategies, they neglect the last link—they sabotage the strategy where it matters most, where the company comes into contact with its customers. They fail to forge the vital connection between strategy and execution at the customer interface, where margins, growth, and profitability are all determined. And yet somehow, companies still expect to see results.

HOW STRATEGY—AND THE ORGANIZATION—CAN SUCCEED

To survive, companies depend on their sales organizations to position and sell the value of their solutions. When salespeople meet their customers, they must translate corporate strategy into effective plans, plans that create the best, most profitable deals possible. If the salespeople don't make deals that connect to the corporate strategy, the company doesn't make its numbers or meet its goals. Profit falls short and the organization is left playing catch-up.

If you can't position and sell your company's product or service profitably when you're face-to-face with your customers, you are dead in the water. No amount of strategic planning, analysis, preparation, product development, customer support, or marketing will get you the results you need if you have not prepared your salespeople to make the sales that create the best results.

Anything less than stellar performance leads to lost or suboptimal sales and will wreak havoc on your bottom line. And the bottom line is the only thing that Wall Street, shareholders, and investors are looking at when they are evaluating and measuring your company's performance.

So what can you do?

For the past twenty-five years, my colleagues and I have worked with some of the best-performing, most respected companies in the world, some marginal performers, and some companies that have fallen from grace. What we've learned is that many experience the gap, the broken link, between having a corporate strategy and executing that strategy where it counts the most: at the point of customer contact. We have also learned what it takes to close that gap and connect strategy and execution in order to increase revenue and optimize margins. Our tried-and-true methods have produced remarkable results:

- A Fortune 50 global communications firm realized a 2-plus percent revenue lift and reduced its overall sales cycle time by more than 35 percent by employing our methods.

- An independent industry analyst reported that our client, a multi-billion-dollar consumer products company, had gone from an average performer to the top 5 percent in its industry group in margins, sales growth, and return on sales.

- Another Fortune 500 client recently reduced their solution discounting by 14 percent in two short quarters, using our strategies and methodologies. Each discount point equated to $12 million in annual profit. Over three quarters, the net increase in profit was just short of $40 million.

- Sales teams in our client organizations, across the board, have become consistently effective at dealing with (and in many cases avoiding) unnecessary giveaways that eroded account profitability.

- On average our clients have shortened their sales cycle time by 27 percent using our comprehensive strategy execution planning tools and methodology.

In this book I will tell you what you need to do to achieve results like these. I am going to lay out the requirements for thinking and acting differently to achieve your corporate strategy in ways that you have not previously considered. I am going to help you rewire the way your sales organization executes your corporate strategy at the point of customer contact.

I will introduce you to foolproof concepts and methods our clients have used over the years to achieve dramatic improvement in their execution of corporate strategy. I will help you apply our concepts, methods, and tools to achieve increased revenue and margin optimization—measures of the success of your corporate strategy. Finally, I will show you how to embed our methodology in your organization so that you have far more control over margin erosion, discounting, and price waterfall—three areas that have a huge impact on your bottom line.

This book is organized to provide you with the information and tools you need to meet the challenges of making your numbers in the modern marketplace:

- Section I: Introduction, which includes this chapter and the next, discusses the critical challenge corporate leadership faces today: closing the gap that exists between the articulation of the corporate strategy and successfully executing that strategy at the point of customer contact.

- Section II: Closing the Gap introduces the concepts, principles, and planning process designed to help your organization execute its corporate strategy at the customer interface.

- Section III: The Unbreakable Chain details how each entity in your organization must contribute to executing corporate strategy at the point of customer contact and then introduces ways to implement the key concepts described in section II.

- The application section provides critical support for the key ideas of the book. Course A presents the business acumen requirements for successfully executing strategy at the point of customer interaction; course B details a comprehensive set of change management principles; and course C gives readers a chance to test their new-found knowledge with a practical exercise.

Are you ready to start getting the results you need to remain competitive and profitable in today's business climate?

Summary

Introduction: The Broken Link

- There is increased pressure in the marketplace to meet your numbers and rapid growth of new challenges to making it happen.

- Cost cutting is no longer a viable option for making your numbers—you must create expanded sales opportunities with expedited sales cycles, create an "insurance policy" for unexpected disruptions in the business environment, and ensure sustained, predictable sales and earnings growth.

- To achieve these goals, you must turn corporate strategy into profitable sales.

- Many organizations lack the ability to carry out their corporate strategy through sales at the point of customer contact, where strategy matters the most.

2

IDENTIFYING THE GAP

Vision without execution is hallucination.
—Thomas Edison

Every day, all over the world, businesspeople struggle to transform top-line strategy into bottom-line results. Over the years, I've watched many companies tackling the thorny challenges of implementing their corporate strategies. Where results have been less than optimal, there are a few key factors that almost always come into play.

In one common pattern, management takes a linear, rational approach to creating the strategy—often with the help of strategic consultants trained in traditional business school methods. Market analyses are performed, performance data is analyzed, problems are identified, goals are agreed upon, and solutions are recommended. From this process, a strategy reflecting management's best thinking on how to deal with the current marketplace in light of the company's strengths and capabilities is born. This is an intelligent approach that should produce results. Right? The problem is that more often than not, once a strategy is set, the necessary thought, planning, and executive support are not deployed to make sure it actually gets carried out.

Researchers have isolated reasons for the mass failure of corporate strategies. They cite lack of time spent actually fulfilling the strategy and even employees' lack of access to the strategy as prime causes. "Eighty-five percent of management teams spend less than one hour per month on strategy issues and only 5 percent of employees understand their corporate strategy," writes Peter S. DeLisi, citing a 1996 Renaissance Solutions survey.[1] "The typical company gives access [to their strategy] to only 42 percent of managers and 27 percent of employees . . . How can we expect employees to be strategic when they do not even have access to the strategy?" asks DeLisi.[2] Employees don't hear about strategy, see it, or know if it's working.

Instead, strategies are talked about at board meetings and shareholder meetings, communicated to Wall Street analysts, and eventually articulated to the employees tasked with executing them. But since most of the emphasis is on the "what" and very little is on the "how," employees all too often return to business as usual. At this key juncture, when management should be instilling the right discipline and giving people the real tools and knowledge they need to execute properly, the focus shifts to other things.

For twenty-five years, I've worked with companies to help them perform better. I've found that many organizations operate in an acceptable manner, but effectively applying corporate strategy to day-to-day business is usually not high on the accomplishment scorecard. What's interesting is that it doesn't matter what the industry is, what the sales organization sells, how the company is organized, or how aggressive the sales team is—the same mistakes are made day in and day out across the board: sales organizations don't prepare their salespeople to execute the company strategy. On that point, I have to paraphrase Thomas Edison's words: strategy without execution is hallucination.

EXECUTING STRATEGY IN THE SALES ORGANIZATION

The sales organization is the crux of a strategy's success. It is the most common place where strategies fail, and more than any other link in the chain, the sales organization has the power to turn strategy into big gains or tragic losses. Each sale either furthers the corporate plan with best-case-scenario deal size, product mixture, profit margin, and contract terms, or represents a lost opportunity or even an unprofitable deal. If strategy gets lost among other concerns in the sales organization, the strategy will fail. And Wall Street, shareholders, investors, and boards of directors are losing their appetite for organizations that lack the ability to execute their plans effectively, because those organizations don't make their numbers.

It's no secret that the cost of failing to execute strategy within the sales organization is increasing. Gone are the days when, if you couldn't make the sale to one division of a global company, you could pick up lost revenue by selling to a different division. In today's marketplace, it's too often an all-or-nothing scenario. And with direct and indirect sales forces often numbering in the thousands and scattered all over the globe, the challenge of managing to get the results you need has become exponentially more complex. Smaller sales forces can present equally difficult challenges, as each rep becomes critically important to the company's success. With the cost of failure increasing and sales management becoming more complex, a clearly communicated and embedded strategy execution plan is more critical than ever.

Lacking a cohesive and consistent game plan, people in selling organizations will work at odds with the strategy and one another. The sales manager and the salespeople may communicate, but often they will talk about the wrong things. For example, the sales manager may encourage salespeople to emphasize product knowledge rather than provide a business solution. The sales rep may make deals without discovering the customer's true needs and constraints. "What's so bad about that?" you ask. "They made a sale. End of story." Wrong. Until you uncover the customer's true needs (as opposed to what he says he wants), clarify how your product solution provides optimal value for the customer, and understand the constraints your customer operates within, you don't know enough to propose and position the best solution possible. And the best solution is the solution that brings your company closer to meeting its strategic goals.

Unprepared salespeople behave reactively instead of proactively; they succumb to price pressure without properly positioning and demonstrating value; they don't prepare sufficiently up front or throughout the sales process; they don't ask for the business at the right time; they give away too much too soon in the sales process; and they talk to customers about products and features rather than solutions. The list goes on, and each profit-killing mistake takes the company farther from its goals. Each mistake costs the company—and the salesperson.

Sales management creates processes they believe will support corporate strategy using tools that are not designed to help execute strategy. The company makes huge investments in ambitious systems, usually customer relationship management (CRM) systems. These systems may help them track aspects of their customer relationships, but more often than not, they don't help users zero in on key business performance and sales metrics, so they can't develop reasonable plans to improve their performance in relation to the corporate strategy. And they don't help salespeople apply the strategy where it counts most: on the front line, selling and negotiating with the customer.

As a result of all of these factors, salespeople do not focus on achieving their company's strategic goals when they interact with customers. That means reduced revenue and lower margins on the sale. All of these profit-killing wrong turns in applying strategy add up over time to create a huge gap—the disconnect between what the strategy is designed to achieve and the actual results you are getting.

As the gap widens, the effect is predictable. Not only does the bottom line erode, but the organization is less agile and reacts to the marketplace slowly; the speed of its response and delivery are compromised. The July 2006 edition of *The McKinsey Quarterly* reported survey findings suggesting that executives and managers across all main regions and industry sectors acknowledge the increasing significance of agility and speed. McKinsey found that survey respondents were convinced they could boost business performance by improving how well their organizations could shift strategic direction and how fast they could execute their operational imperatives.[3] Leaders can gain a distinct competitive advantage if they are able to eliminate the sluggishness that overtakes businesses when they can't connect sales to their strategy.

What if you could close the gap? What would it mean to your organization to eliminate all the wrong turns and increase speed and agility?

THE SALES STRATEGY EXECUTION LANDSCAPE

When management considers how to close the gap to achieve the right results for its organization, it is important to understand the entire sales strategy execution landscape (fig. 2-1). Successful strategy execution can only happen if you first deploy a coherent sales strategy that empowers your salespeople to properly manage the interface with their customers. To be successful, that sales strategy must incorporate clear directives on opportunity management and sales process management. These are the elements that create an environment that will support successful, profitable sales.

Opportunity management enables sales leaders and professionals to use data effectively to qualify a potential client and determine if there is a true opportunity to win the customer's business. This component of sales strategy requires that you conduct research and collect data that will help you understand the customer's business, identifying where your company's solution may fit and how much value it could provide. Successful opportunity management is reliant upon understanding the competition you are facing and how your solution could help your customer create a competitive advantage in the marketplace. Finally, it requires a plan for leveraging your value proposition and determining what the time-to-revenue will be if you move the sale forward.

Sales process management is all about collecting and using data, which includes evaluating your customer's buying process, mapping the sales process specific to the opportunity, and determining who the key influencers and decision makers are. You must develop provocative questions to ask your customer, plan when to ask them, and create response positions

FIGURE 2-1   *There is a gap, or disconnect, between the strategy to achieve initiatives and execution of the strategy at the customer interface.*

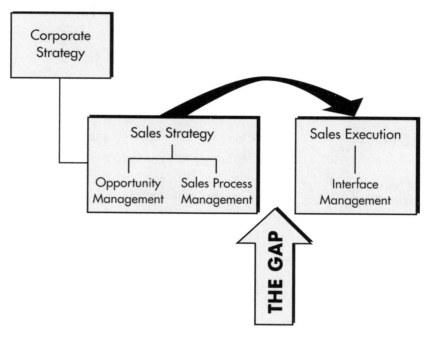

in anticipation of how your customer may respond. Sales process management also includes framing and creating position themes focused on making the key agreements connected to the amount of revenue and degree of profitability the sale will result in.

While opportunity management and sales process management are critical to the overall success of sales strategy, once you understand those elements, it's time to execute and have planned results-oriented dialogue with your customer. The point of execution is the focus of this book because that is the point where most strategies fail—or succeed. This point is interface management, and it is the last link.

THE LAST LINK: INTERFACE MANAGEMENT

Interface management is leveraging the knowledge you've built to execute the most optimal deal when face-to-face with your customer. It is the most important component of successful sales strategy execution. Throughout the rest of this book, I will outline the knowledge, concepts, and methods you need to close the gap and execute profitable sales through successful interface management. I am going to help you connect strategy to bottom-line results by showing you how to rewire the way your sales organization thinks about and applies its sales practices. Through discipline, you can embed key concepts and methods that will result in successful interface management:

- *Pivotal Agreements* are agreements made with customers throughout the sales process that are connected to the financial metrics of your corporate strategy—and therefore to your company's strategic goals. They have significant, direct impact on the ultimate outcome of your sales process.

- The *3D Model* represents the winning combination of gathering relevant data, using focused dialogue, and executing strategy with discipline. These 3 Ds—data, dialogue, and discipline—are essential to closing the gap.

- The *Dialogue Principles* are the key tactics for managing the customer interface to make sure your customer understands the value of your solution and to develop the best possible agreements for the company and the client.

- The *Sales Execution Plan* is a written document that defines an organization's specific plans for executing corporate strategy at the point of customer interface. It explains how the company will apply the 3D Model and the Dialogue Principles to successfully negotiate the Pivotal Agreements that are essential to a successful final sale.

- The final element is to successfully integrate the strategy through deployment, sponsorship, and reinforcement of discipline by senior executives and the leadership team.

If you are ready to learn how to close the gap that is sabotaging your business, read on.

Summary

Introduction: Identifying the Gap

- When management doesn't require the implementation of a focused strategy at the point of customer contact, sales are made that don't support the strategy.

- This gap leads to reduced revenue and lower profit margins.

- To close the gap, you must rewire the way your sales organization thinks about and executes its sales practices.

CLOSING THE GAP

3

PIVOTAL AGREEMENTS AND THE 3D MODEL

The way to close the gap between your corporate strategy and the results you seek is to execute effectively.

OK, you say to yourself, I've got a corporate strategy. It's focused on growth, increasing market share, improving speed and agility in the marketplace, introducing new technologies, and selling profitable product mixes. It's been properly launched: you've given the speeches, had the meetings, and implemented the tools. But a fundamental disconnect continues between what you need to have happen and what's actually going on in your organization. You're pushing out new technologies, but the market has not been quick to embrace them. Your customers are pushing back on price and you find you're booking less profitable business. The majority of your sales are exception based and your deal approvers have a chokehold on closes. Sales cycle time has increased, your customers seem less satisfied, and rather than increasing market share, you're in jeopardy of losing what you've got.

Why is success eluding you? How do you fix it? That's what this section of the book is about.

The system works like this: first, you must identify the right agreements, particularly the right Pivotal Agreements, that you need to make to advance the sale to the best, most profitable close. Then you must apply the principles in the 3D Model—data, dialogue, and discipline—to making each agreement. When you use this method, you will optimize the size and profitability of each deal you make (fig. 3-1).

THE PIVOTAL NATURE OF AGREEMENTS

When most sales professionals and their managers think of agreements, they have a clear picture in their minds: the final contract that closes the business. This shouldn't be a surprise. After all, that's the agreement they're measured and compensated upon.

However, a common and costly misconception (often driven by managers focused excessively on deal closure) is that the size and profitability of

FIGURE 3-1   *Executing Pivotal Agreements using the 3D Model—data, dialogue, and discipline—leads to opimized sales.*

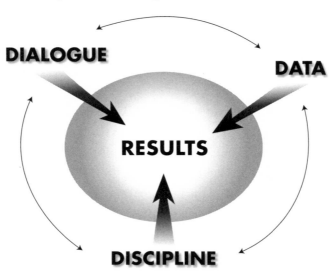

the deal results from the action that salespeople take at the final stages of the sales cycle, when the contract is finalized. This belief may seem intuitively correct, but it creates a significant disadvantage for a sales team looking for ways to improve deal size and account profitability. Those kinds of results can only occur if the right agreements are identified and negotiated much earlier in the sales process. Great sales result from the effective execution of agreements throughout the customer engagement process. In fact, you could look at the sales process as building and crafting a series of agreements, both with your customer and with people inside your own organization.

A leader who insists salespeople only focus on the closing process is like a golf pro who tells a student to focus only on his drives off of the tee, since the length of the tee shot moves the player closer to the hole. Anybody who plays golf or has watched it on television knows that a player only makes par if he executes a series of shots well: the drive up the fairway, the approach onto the green, and ultimately the final putt. The quality of each shot has a cumulative effect on the final score.

It's the same in sales. Each incremental agreement you make throughout the sales process contributes to the size, quality, and profitability of the final contract. The ultimate deal is the sum of all the agreements made between the first customer contact and a signed contract. But not all agreements are equal. During any sales process, there are usually a dozen or so key agreements that will determine the size and profitability of the sale. These agreements are different for every company, but they almost always involve questions of access, risk, technical issues, economic considerations, value, scheduling, and price.

Any given company's customer engagement process might require crafting hundreds of agreements. But typically there are no more than six to eight agreements that dictate the ultimate success or failure of the sales process and the corporate strategy: the Pivotal Agreements.

Pivotal Agreements are the agreements that are connected to the financial metrics of your corporate strategy—and therefore to the company's strategic goals. They have significant, direct impact on the ultimate outcome of your sales process, especially as it relates to hitting profitability and revenue goals. Making these agreements and making them well leads to profitable, advantageous, solution-based sales. Not identifying and making these Pivotal Agreements jeopardizes the size and profitability of the ultimate deal, and often can result in no deal at all.

Because they are connected to the financial metrics of your corporate strategy, Pivotal Agreements are specific to each organization and solution set, and generally yield 80 percent or more of the results you measure for. Unfortunately, companies rarely identify the Pivotal Agreements throughout their own sales processes, as it requires sophisticated expertise to do this effectively. However, this is a skill that can be taught. When asked "What is a Pivotal Agreement in your sales process?" most salespeople will answer, "Getting the customer to sign the contract." But think about it: successfully closing an optimal contract agreement usually follows successfully crafting a series of earlier, equally important, Pivotal Agreements that determine the terms, scope, profitability, and content of the contract. Some areas that form the basis for Pivotal Agreements include

- Identifying key decision makers and a strategy to connect with them
- Developing a process for tracking compliance with key contract terms and conditions
- Accessing appropriate documentation to provide the highest-value solution at the best price
- Understanding the client's full need for a complete solution set, rather than just understanding what they say they initially want
- Creating a well thought out concession strategy for dealing with price pressure

Obviously, the ultimate success of a sales organization depends on its ability to execute quality agreements that lead to greater market share and profits. To achieve the best results on metrics such as discount level, account margin, and sales cycle speed, salespeople need to be able to do two things. First, they must be able to position the value of the product or service they are selling in terms that resonate powerfully with the customer. Second, they must be able to show how the purchase of the product or service will contribute directly to the customer's ability to meet his or her own corporate goals (e.g., increase profit, improve customer service, develop and deliver superior products and services, etc.). Agreements that result from this kind of positioning are value-based agreements. Your sales force should be working on building these sorts of agreements with their customers and within their own organization at each step in the customer engagement process.

At most companies the customer engagement process includes a half dozen or more Pivotal Agreements, each of which must be handled well if the sales team hopes to close profitable final contracts with customers. At one telecommunications company I worked with, management's goal was to increase average deal size and get larger "share of wallet" (i.e., a higher percentage of the customer's telecommunications budget) in their highly competitive industry. They had conducted comprehensive product and sales training and engaged in far-ranging advertising and promotion activity to make this happen. But because they did not have the right sales execution strategy in place, they concluded that the only way to accomplish their goal was through extensive, costly discounting. An analysis of the company's Pivotal Agreements showed that the size and scope of final customer contracts were determined much earlier in the sales process, when the best account executives got their buyers to agree to

- Give them data about their current and future telecommunications growth needs, especially globally (where the company had a distinct competitive value advantage), before talking about pricing

- Let them interview the users of telecommunications services (such as the heads of sales and operations) rather than limiting access to telecommunications managers; this pivotal agreement created an opportunity for account executives to validate the importance of network reliability, an area in which they surpassed all other providers

- Let them bring in members of their professional services consulting team early in the sales process (which would often result in expanding the scope of implementation and sometimes result in additional managed services contracts)

- Get the company's purchasing managers to defer premature price pressure to give the account execs time to collect more data about the customer's overall telecommunication needs; this in turn created the opportunity to sell their true competitive value (the reliability of their network)

When the sales team focused on these agreements as well as final contract negotiations, their success improved dramatically. In fact, this company conducted an internal study comparing sales teams that had been exposed to this approach to those that hadn't been and found that focusing on successfully executing those Pivotal Agreements led to an overall increase of average revenue of more than 2 percent. This 2 percent revenue lift translated to more than $100 million in revenue on an annualized basis.

Of course, the Pivotal Agreements that drive strategy execution vary from company to company and from organization to organization within each company, based on how each company sells, the nature of its value proposition, and the nature of its products or services. Regardless of what your Pivotal Agreements are, however, I can assure you that when you make them, timing is critical. Let me explain.

In a classic six-step sales process you typically qualify your prospect, engage in a "discovery" process to uncover needs, meet and present your solution, make a proposal, draw up a contract, and close the sale. A number of pivotal moments present themselves throughout the sales cycle, during which you determine the results of your sale. Figure 3-2 lists the Pivotal Agreements we helped one client identify. As a result of making these Pivotal Agreements in approximately 36 percent of their sales during the first three months of the initiative, this organization increased revenue 11.9 percent. As you can see, the majority of the Pivotal Agreements had to occur early on in the sales process. This timing structure applies across most industries and in most sales situations. That means that if you have

FIGURE 3-2 *In optimal sales execution, Pivotal Agreements are typically made early in the sales process.*

Sample Pivotal Agreement

	Sales Process					
	Step 1 Qualify	Step 2 Discover	Step 3 Meet/Present	Step 4 Propose	Step 5 Contract	Step 6 Close
Access to large deal qualifying data	X	X				
Sponsor's commitment to organization-wide deployment	X	X	X			
Getting commitment to internal data collection/reporting to uncover full sales opportunities	X	X	X			
Ongoing executive access/commitment to maintain sponsorship	X		X			
Endorsement of rapid/deep deployment of our solution		X				
Initial rollout success criteria leading to organization-wide deployment of our solution		X	X	X		
Agreement to use our paper for contract		X	X			
Contractual agreement to monitor compliance with volume & payment terms		X	X	X	X	X

not identified your Pivotal Agreements and determined how you will make them while planning the sales process—before your first call—you are not going to make the best sale possible.

Of course, you can blow a Pivotal Agreement and still close a deal. But the value of your deal will be needlessly diminished and will likely cost your company significant real dollars. Since each Pivotal Agreement represents a fork in the road in the sales process, the direction you take will affect the outcome. If you make a good Pivotal Agreement, you'll end up higher on the profitability scale. If you make a mediocre Pivotal Agreement, you'll still close the business, but you'll be leaving money on the table. If you make a poor Pivotal Agreement, you'll be leaving even more money on the table. Figure 3-3 lays out some examples of Pivotal Agreements across industries.

Sometimes the subtleties of Pivotal Agreements are not obvious. For example, an energy company we've worked with sells its energy-saving services to government agencies and public institutions. An analysis of their Pivotal Agreements shows that some critical agreements are not obvious at first.

> Obvious: get the data to create a winning proposal.
> Not so obvious: get government workers to help you uncover precisely what critical data you need.
>
> Obvious: get the governing entity (the board or city council) to vote "yes" on the solution.
> Not so obvious: get the input and support of key government officials before the vote is taken.

When looking for Pivotal Agreements, you must focus on the whole customer engagement process. Agreements can arise in a service context as well as during the selling process. For example, when a major cable TV company looked for moments in their expanded sales process when they were most likely to get favorable agreements to buy more services, they determined that one such moment was when their installer arrived to turn on the service that had already been sold. The pivotal customer agreement

FIGURE 3-3   *Pivotal Agreements that drive strategy execution*

Company/ Industry	Goal/Strategy	Example of a Pivotal Agreement That Determines Execution Success or Failure
International telecommunications company	Improve gross margin by 11 percent by reducing average discount by 1 percent.	Can we get the chief information officer to agree to defer price discussions early in the sales cycle so we can fully explore *all* ways we can add value?
Transportation and shipping company	Increase average relationship size by 20 percent by selling logistics solutions rather than just package shipping.	Will the customer give us access to key people during the "needs exploration" stage so we can build their support and sponsorship for our solution?
Enterprise software company that sells to government agencies	Increase sales growth rate by 5 percent by increasing close ratio.	Can we influence the specifications of buyer requests for proposal and avoid costly sales processes that result in losing business to "wired" competitors?
Global consumer products and manufacturing company	Recover $200-plus million in lost profitability by minimizing postsale "margin leakage."	Can the sales team achieve profitable outcomes when faced with margin-eroding postsale negotiations, such as "Who pays for expedited shipping?" or "Will the customer get a full rebate even though they didn't meet their annual volume commitment?"

prompted a buy decision for a higher-level package. The positioning: "I see you have sports memorabilia all around your TV room. If you like sports you should try the ESPN sports package. I can turn it on right now."

Every company's Pivotal Agreements are different. But in all cases the phenomenon is the same: when sales professionals identify and plan out how they will handle Pivotal Agreements, they dramatically increase the odds of winning larger and more profitable deals—and the odds of advancing the numbers that measure strategic success.

How do sales professionals optimize Pivotal Agreements? They apply the principles of the 3D Model—data, dialogue, and discipline—to their selling practice.

THE 3D STRATEGY EXECUTION MODEL

We have found that best-in-class sales organizations combine an astute grasp and use of three critical competencies: (1) relevant data; (2) purposeful, focused dialogue, internally and with customers; and (3) disciplined strategy execution up and down the sales organization. This winning combination creates a strong foundation for compelling, measurable results (fig. 3-4).

How do high-performing sales organizations use data, dialogue, and discipline to close the gap between their corporate strategy and profitable execution of sales with customers? As you'll see in the next three chapters, they

- Collect, analyze, and share pertinent data and metrics among all members of the sales team. This includes quantitative data about sales results, but goes much further. They also share data on how successful they have been in executing the critical customer agreements that help their sales team move profitably through each step in the sales process, and "best practice" data on how to handle predictable challenges in the sales process that affect the success of their corporate strategy.

- Engage in ongoing, purposeful dialogue with everyone who has customer contact and either leads or supports the sales effort. This ensures that salespeople have consistent feedback and a model to help them do and say the right things for the best results at each stage in the sales process. Traditional sales training often teaches people

FIGURE 3-4   *The 3D Model*

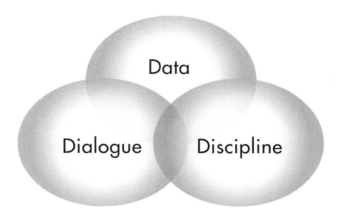

to focus on the wrong things, leaving them ill equipped to optimize sales opportunities. High-performing sales organizations focus their teams on preparing for and having the right dialogues and applying the often counterintuitive Dialogue Principles.

- Instill discipline in their sales organizations. Discipline means holding people accountable for following a strategy execution process as part of a daily sales preparation and sales execution routine tailored to their selling organization. An organization with discipline focuses on making deals that fulfill the corporate strategy, and measures whether people are complying with strategic procedures or not. It reinforces its discipline with communication throughout all levels of the organization.

Many organizations are good in one, perhaps two, of these areas. For example, many technology companies are excellent at analyzing data and structuring disciplined sales processes, but they fall behind in the dialogue component. I believe successful strategy execution at the point of customer interface comes from the interaction of all three: data, dialogue, and discipline.

It's the leaders' role to ensure that all three components are present and interacting. This simple, powerful execution model works in any organization, provided management has the will and leadership to implement it. In the next three chapters, I'll take you on an in-depth tour of the three Ds.

Summary

Closing the Gap: Pivotal Agreements and the 3D Model

- Great sales result from effective execution of a series of agreements that take place throughout the customer engagement process.

- Pivotal Agreements are agreements that are connected to the financial aims and metrics of your corporate strategy. Therefore, they have a significant, direct impact on the ultimate outcome of your sales process, especially as it relates to hitting profitability and revenue goals.

- Every company's Pivotal Agreements are different. People at all levels of a sales organization can optimize Pivotal Agreements by applying the principles of the 3D Model—data, dialogue, and discipline—in their selling practice.

- To succeed, organizations must apply all three principles:
  - o Collect, analyze, and share pertinent data and metrics among the entire sales team.
  - o Engage everyone involved in purposeful dialogue to execute sales strategy at the customer interface.
  - o Instill discipline in the sales organization.

4

DATA

Knowing where you stand means knowing where to go.

Data. We're either collecting it, analyzing it, slicing and dicing it, or reporting it. Data is the first element of the 3D Model (fig. 4-1). Why is data so critical? Because when you have the right kind of data about your customer you can shape the value proposition of your product or service. You can manage the sales process and potential relationship from a position of knowledge and, therefore, strength.

Data comes in many forms from many sources. Annual reports, strategic initiative statements, investor reports, and trade and business magazines are all great sources of information—as is talking directly to the customer and their suppliers. Your salespeople are undoubtedly adept at collecting and analyzing data about their prospects and customers. And as a result, your sales force understands their customers well enough to know how to position your products or service to show how it will help them meet

FIGURE 4-1 *The 3D Model: Data*

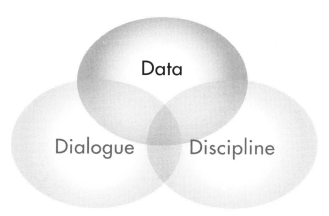

their objectives. However, they need more data to help them execute your company's strategy.

Your company, like many others, may have made sizable investments in data gathering systems like customer relationship management (CRM) software. As a result, you know a great deal more about your sales process: the length of the sales cycle, the outcome of forecasted opportunities, and the number of calls it takes to close a sale. So you know a great deal more about your customers: what they buy, how frequently they buy it, and what their price tolerance is.

If you have that kind of information, theoretically that means you have a handle on all the key data points and are in a position to use that data to optimize sales. That's why you collect the data any way you can. That's why you've got your salespeople chasing down information that gives them insight into their customers' goals, needs, and buying behavior. That's why you bought a CRM tool or related system, trained your people on it, and implemented it into your organization—at great cost.

So why is there still a gap? How can data be a weak spot?

In my experience, companies aren't able to use data effectively to optimize sales for three reasons:

1. They track the wrong data. We've seen that while sales leadership tracks metrics that are related to their corporate strategy, they often

don't track data that yields the precise information they need to execute more profitable sales. For example, at a consumer products company, the corporate strategy was to improve gross margins. They dutifully tracked margins down to the regional level; then they put all their reps through sales training and waited for the margins to go up. Unfortunately, they were not able to track individual account profitability by product, so regional management wasn't able to effectively manage the team to create better sales results.

2. The data they do track isn't actionable. Companies often do well at tracking data, but they don't know what to do with it after it's collected. The data isn't converted into a form that lends itself to the kind of analysis that leads to solid conclusions and decisions about what needs to happen.

3. Data does not get into the hands of the right people. Companies may have the data and even perform the right analyses, but typically the people who are actually in face-to-face conversations with customers don't receive the data or the analysis. Without easy access to that information, salespeople are unable to have constructive dialogues with their customers that can optimize sales opportunities. As one impassioned sales executive said to me, "Those people who look into the customer's eyes must have the appropriate information to drive gross margin improvement."

When the right data isn't tracked, made actionable, and put into the hands of the right people, sales go awry. For example, take the case of a communications company that set its corporate strategy to increase top- and bottom-line growth. They only tracked revenue growth, and so had no way to measure whether or not they were succeeding on their margins. Because they didn't track margin results on a sale-by-sale basis, they had no idea if and when they were closing unprofitable sales. Unknown to the company and its sales organization, the salespeople were bowing to pressure in a commodity-driven marketplace and selling at any price. They kept cutting their prices and booking unprofitable business, unwittingly sabotaging the bottom line. If the organization had been able to sell their highly differentiated value proposition effectively and track their margins—by product, by customer—and put that information, along with the appropriate sales execution skills, processes, and tools, into the hands of their salespeople, they could have reversed their downward spiral. Instead, their revenues slightly increased, but their margins eroded dramatically. Consequently, they did not hit their revenue goals and their horrible margin performance led to an employee layoff.

To attain the results you desire, you need to think about your data differently. For the purposes of achieving your strategy, that means tracking the right data and getting it into the hands of the people who can move the numbers in the right direction.

WHAT ARE YOU LEAVING ON THE TABLE?

Do you ever wonder what your salespeople leave on the table after they conclude a negotiation? Did they get the best possible price? Did they optimize margins by minimizing unnecessary discounts and giveaways?

You already know that it is critical to manage price. Experts at McKinsey and Company studied price management practices and concluded there were enormous gains to be made.

> Pricing right is the fastest and most effective way for managers to increase profits. Consider the average income statement of an S&P 1500 company: a price rise of 1 percent, if volumes remained stable, would generate an 8 percent increase in operating profits.[1]

What you might not know is that if you aren't getting the best price, you're not only missing an opportunity to improve operating profits, you're also forcing yourself to play catch-up by generating a staggering amount of sales just to make up for the erosion in price. The report continues,

> Managers may hope that higher volumes will compensate for revenues lost from lower prices and thereby raise profits, but this rarely happens . . . A strategy based on cutting prices to increase volumes and, as a result, to raise profits is generally doomed to failure in almost every market and industry.[2]

You already know you need to manage your margins. You don't want to give away anything more than is necessary to close a deal. What you might not know is that discounts, giveaways, and concessions have a tendency to add up and create a phenomenon known as "price waterfall"—a profit killer hidden in layers of deal discount iterations and back-and-forth negotiation (fig. 4-2).

A number of management consulting firms work with companies to develop price waterfall analyses for them. The goal is to determine the company's pocket price—the amount left from a sale when discounts, rebates, and other concessions, many of which are "unearned," are subtracted from typical list and invoice prices. In the example in figure 4-2, you can see the dramatic decline from list price to pocket price when you track all the costs associated with discounts, giveaways, and concessions.

How much is your sales force giving away—in payment terms, discounts, annual volume bonuses, off-invoice promotions, co-op advertising, and freight—when they negotiate deals? That you do not know about? That you are not measuring? That you are not tracking? That leads to a price waterfall?

These and many other factors contribute to potential revenue and margin leakage. There are concessions that transfer risks and burdens to sellers in negotiated commercial terms that have a cost, but are not measured or tracked, because they represent contingencies only—for example, indemnities, liability caps, and warranty extensions. I can guarantee that if you're not managing all or most of these factors to your advantage, your experienced customers are going to work them to theirs. And if you're not tracking the right data, chances are you won't even know that it's happening.

Identifying and tracking the right data and using the data in planning the execution of your sales strategy is an important step on your journey to controlling pocket price erosion and minimizing the price waterfall. But that data won't be actionable until you use it in the context of agreements you need to make throughout the sales process to move the sale toward a profitable close.

FIGURE 4-2 *Discounts, giveaways, and concessions lead to price waterfall.*

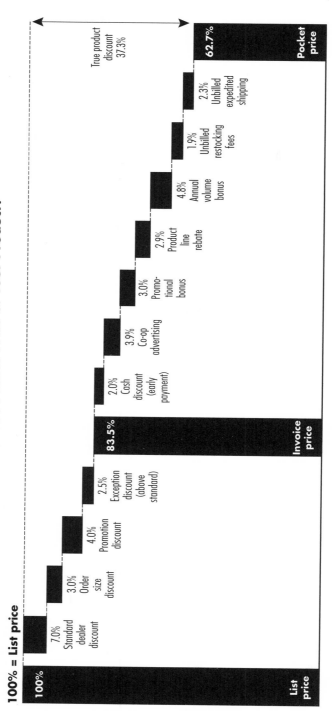

Price Waterfall Analysis:
What Is the True Pocket Price of Your Product?

DATA THAT MATTERS: UNDERSTANDING
AND MANAGING THE METRICS OF PIVOTAL AGREEMENTS

There are all kinds of variables you must manage to create successful sales outcomes: positioning your product or service, price, discounts, margins, invoice price, pocket price, length of sales cycle, contract terms, and customer compliance, to name a few. And there are varying degrees to which a sales organization can control these variables. For example, at a major consumer products organization, the sales representatives are not authorized to negotiate price. But they can negotiate on just about anything else: product mix, displays, freshness of supply, return agreements, shipping agreements, and so on. Not only does their sales organization have control over these things, but how they manage these variables has a direct effect on the margins of the deal.

So, how do you manage the variables that have significant bearing on the outcome of the sale to the best of your ability? It starts with tracking and reporting the metrics that are connected to Pivotal Agreements.

Managers and sales teams can close the gap between strategy and successful sales execution by understanding and managing to the metrics of the Pivotal Agreements that must be made to optimize the deal. It should come as no surprise that companies can (and should) collect and analyze metrics related to agreements, especially Pivotal Agreements, made during the customer engagement process. The most useful metrics are those that relate to results (dollars booked) or process ("Did I get to the decision maker early in the sales cycle?").

Here is an example of how a consumables manufacturing company effectively used data and metrics. Their corporate strategy focused on increasing relationship size and account profitability through a combination of market segmentation and a new contracting approach. The problem: their buyers had become accustomed to the old contracting approach, which had been in place for several years. To make their strategy work with their customers, the company analyzed its sales process and determined that they needed to make two Pivotal Agreements that had not been made before: one to get the customer to agree to use the new contracting method, and one to get the customer to comply with the terms of the contract.

Ultimately, sales leadership identified and tracked two process metrics: the percentage of customers using the new contracting method, and the percentage of customers who were contract compliant. Then they implemented two annual sales meetings focused on preparing the sales team to identify and complete Pivotal Agreements. The meetings helped the salespeople use data about their customers to develop and implement Sales Execution Plans to move customers to the new contract model and move the metrics in the right direction.

The proof was in the pudding. Two years later, independent industry analysts reported that this company had risen from an average performer to the top 20 percent in its industry in margins, sales growth, and return on sales.

THE TWO CATEGORIES OF DATA YOU NEED TO TRACK

Every organization's metrics are different. But as you analyze the dynamics of your unique environment, there are two major types of metrics that you should be tracking and measuring:

1. **Results metrics**: These are "scorecard data" that reflect outcomes: for example, gross revenue, gross margins, product sales, customer buying history, and the like. Results metrics tell you how you did—like looking through a rearview mirror, it shows you things after the fact. But if all you have is historical data, you don't have what you need to manage future results. And that's where process metrics come into play.

2. **Process metrics**: These are leading process indicators that represent the things that have to get done to achieve the results you want. If you apply these metrics consistently over time, you know you're going to get the results you're looking for. For example, when the stock market indexes increase, the market is signaling that the prospect for future corporate earnings has increased.

Both of these types of metrics can be used in their own unique ways to help you evaluate your sales processes.

RESULTS METRICS

There are two categories of results metrics: performance indicators and customer metrics.

Performance Indicators

Performance indicators are results metrics that link directly to revenue and margins. Typical performance indicators are

- Sales growth
- Sales growth by product
- Margin, by customer and perhaps by product line
- Percentage discount

If you were to identify the most important measures of your performance and list some metrics you could track that would show how well you accomplished what you set out to do, it might resemble figure 4-3.

One leading business software company has a corporate strategy focused on improving account margins and deepening customer relationships. Rather than simply measuring revenue volume, this company focuses on two results metrics:

1. Average invoice discount (which reflects account profitability), and

2. Average number of different applications sold per relationship (which quantifies depth of customer relationship).

Here's how a major consumer products company used metrics to minimize margin leakage. Their go-to-market strategy focused on improving profitability by minimizing margin erosion throughout the sales and ongoing service process. They conducted a division-by-division price

FIGURE 4-3   *Measuring performance indicators*

Performance Indicator	Typical Metrics
Increase revenue	• Overall revenue level improvement • Revenue per customer, per relationship, per deal • Contract renewal performance • Customer overall margin as compared with other customers
Enlarge customer relationship size	• Share of wallet (percentage of total budget that your organization wins) • Cross-sell performance: solution vs. single product sales
Reduce discounting	• Discount off list price • Percent of deals closed above walkaway target • Margin on sales • Average percent of authorized price at which the deal closed
Reduce margin leakage	• Pocket price/margin leakage reduction (for example, the percent of deals with full price service, shipping, etc.) • Contract compliance: percentage of compliance to terms and conditions, volume commitments, etc.
Shorten sales cycles	• Escalation cycle time (for example, number of iterations required from submission of special discount request to approval of the final agreed-on price) • Cycle time from lead to closed contract • Proposal to close cycle time

waterfall analysis to determine where the most significant margin erosion was taking place. They discovered that although they could reduce discounts, they could also recover significant margin by focusing the sales team on other areas, including

- Minimizing the number of times customers requested and received unreimbursed, expedited "free" shipping

- Not giving customers "under 30 days" early payment discounts when they actually paid their invoices on a normal 30- to 45-day schedule

- Managing the insurance and other costs related to customers who delayed taking delivery of product even though it was sitting by their factories in rail cars waiting to be unloaded

Identifying and tracking the metrics associated with profit leakage was a critical step toward turning the situation around. Armed with precise knowledge about each customer's past leakages, the sales force was able to focus on ways to execute better agreements both during the initial contracting process and during the course of ongoing account management. The results: the sales team became more effective at dealing with (and in many cases avoiding) unnecessary giveaways that eroded account profitability.

Once you isolate and track the results metrics that support your corporate strategy, you are ready to identify the Pivotal Agreements that correspond to them. In figure 4-4, I have listed several sample Pivotal Agreements that will have a direct impact on moving the results metrics in the right direction.

Customer Metrics

Customer metrics reveal the details of your relationships with your customers. They can tell you whether your relationships are troubled, profitable, problematic, fair, or high-maintenance.

There are two distinct types of customer metrics you should be collecting. One set of metrics relates to how your customers make their buy decisions and negotiate their purchases. Information about the strategies, tactics, and logistics customers use when buying and negotiating is invaluable when it comes to establishing a winning position theme and identifying the Pivotal Agreements that need to be made to advance the sale toward a profitable close. Unfortunately, that kind of data is rarely gathered, understood, or shared.

The other set of customer metrics gives you information about how your customers are performing in current agreements. Some customer metrics you might consider tracking are

FIGURE 4-4   *Pivotal Agreements that will "move the metrics" to achieve the corporate strategy*

A. Leading Software Company

Corporate Strategy	Metrics	Sample Pivotal Agreements
Improving account margins and deepening customer relationships	• Average invoice discount (which reflects account profitability) • Average number of different applications sold per relationship (which quantifies depth of customer relationship)	• Agreement with executive representing software user population to share data on business needs and user requirements • Buyer agreement to allow completion of a comprehensive user audit (to uncover needs for a wider array of software tools)

B. Major Consumer Products Company

Corporate Strategy	Metrics	Sample Pivotal Agreements
Improving profitability by minimizing margin leakage throughout the sales and ongoing services process	• Minimizing the number of times customers requested and received unreimbursed expedited shipping • Not giving customers "under 30 days" early payment discounts (when they in fact paid their invoices on a normal 30- to 45-day schedule) • Managing demurrage (the insurance and other costs related to customers who delayed taking delivery of product even though it was sitting by their factories in rail cars waiting to be unloaded)	• Agreement to an annual, detailed review of contract terms/conditions • Agreement to quarterly service quality review with customer (which includes discussion of contract compliance performance issues that affect margin) • Completion of contract (or contract renewal) with clear terms/conditions in areas with historical margin leakage • Agreement when exceptions to contract arise to exchange value (rather than expect us to give a concession without getting one in return)

- Customer requests for expedited shipping that they don't pay for
- How well customers are complying with the volume commitments they made in current contracts

The customer metrics you need to track are highly individual and depend on the nature of your business. Rest assured, however, that having an in-depth understanding of your customer metrics and putting that information in the hands of a salesperson trained to execute strategy effectively can have a huge impact on your bottom line.

Look what happened when one of our clients, a snack food manufacturing business, put the right customer metrics in the hands of their sales professionals.

> We put a lot of pieces into place to measure return on investment on a promotion-by-promotion basis. As a result, all of our [salespeople] now have support mechanisms to look at ROI analyses on their accounts . . . And that ROI information gets plugged right into our negotiations on future programs with our customers . . . We can now say to our customer "You committed a volume of X to us . . . and what you actually delivered was 20 percent less." Now that really gives us something significant to talk about with the customer. And that's really where a lot of the negotiation occurs.

PROCESS METRICS

Process metrics measure the efficiency and effectiveness of any process you have in place to create sales—the actions that lead to end results, but aren't outcomes in and of themselves. When you identify process metrics and actively engage your sales force in improving their performance on specific process metrics, you are setting the stage for positive change. In figure 4-5, I have listed two sample Pivotal Agreements that will have a direct impact on moving the process metrics in the right direction. Some useful process metrics—and what they help you measure—are listed in figure 4-6.

Process metrics can be a useful tool in helping your company achieve your corporate strategy. A software company we worked with was determined

FIGURE 4-5   *Pivotal Agreements that will "move the metrics" to achieve
the corporate strategy*

Leading Software Company		
Corporate Strategy	**Metric**	**Sample Pivotal Agreements**
Improving account margins and deepening customer relationships	• Percentage of deals that close before the second month of a quarter (a measure of how well the salesperson avoids "end of quarter" negotiation tactics from buyers)	• Agreement of purchasing and legal to a proposed schedule of contract review and release of purchase order • Agreement of executive sponsor to intercede with purchasing when needed to expedite contracting

to get their discounting under control. We knew we had to go beyond traditional measures of general revenue growth, product revenue growth, or overall margins to help them positively affect their problem. An extensive analysis yielded an interesting fact: their discounting was heavily affected by when in the quarter the deal closed. They realized that if they closed a deal early in the quarter, the profitability of the deal went up because the discounts were lower.

They began to track a key process metric: the percentage of deals closed in the first two months of the quarter. When management focused attention on this metric, it led to new behavior on the part of the sales representatives. The sales representatives and their managers analyzed their sales process and determined that the timing of the buy process was a Pivotal Agreement they needed to make with their customers. Armed with this insight, sales reps started positioning the value of closing the deal earlier in the quarter.

Understanding how to manage this process metric paid off: more deals closed earlier in the quarter rather than later when the price pressure was most severe. Discounting was dramatically reduced.

FIGURE 4-6   *Measuring process metrics*

Process Metrics	Help You Measure
Number of "advances" from Step A to Step B in the sales process this month	Speed of sales cycle
Number of monthly sales execution team meetings held, broken out by manager	Manager compliance with deal management discipline
Number of individual coaching sessions, broken out by manager	Manager reinforcement of effective strategy execution discipline
Number of deals in pipeline above $250K that have reached favorable Pivotal Agreement(s)	Likelihood of closing business that supports the corporate strategy profitably
Number of deal escalations received by marketing that have documented Sales Execution Plans attached	Likelihood that unusually priced deals will be negotiated profitably
Days it takes to close a sales cycle (aimed at reducing cycle time)	Sales cycle time
Number of personnel hours spent on scoping and specifying solutions	Profitability of sales process
Number of customer visits to close the sale (aimed at reducing number of sales calls)	Sales cycle time
Number of agreements made early in the sales cycle that affect close time and profitability of sale	Sales process efficiency
Number of times best practices data was accessed and used	Compliance of sales team to the use of best practices to improve sales results
Number of communication opportunities taken that link the corporate strategy with the sales strategy to complete the right agreements	Reinforcement of the company's strategy execution discipline
Percentage of contracts closed by end of second month in quarter	Likelihood of optimizing discount levels

BEST PRACTICES METRICS

Best practices are the "how to" knowledge that sales teams need to understand in order to make the results metrics, specifically performance indicators, move in the right direction. You not only have to know what your best practices are, you have to share them.

Paul F. Kocourek, Walter J. Mancini, and Matthew Calderone report, "Companies that effectively share best practices have boosted their bottom lines by as much as 20 percent. In a world where the competition is ever increasing, an effective best practices program can prove to be a powerful tool for driving world-class performance."[3]

The challenge with best practices is to make them as specific as possible so that salespeople can take the right action once they are aware of them. To make the needle move on metrics like sales volume, sales cycle speed, won-lost business, and discounting performance, it is important to understand in detail the best practices used by top performers to execute agreements, particularly Pivotal Agreements, at every point in the sales process, and to embed them into the organization's deal management system.

When you identify the agreements that determine the quality of the sale and track the metrics that are linked to them, you can identify best practices. Your inventory of best practices might include things like

- How to position your value so that the buying organization is eager to give you access to their senior executives early in your sales process

- Examples of negotiables you might trade to get your customer to agree to let you present your proposal to the economic buyer instead of a recommender

- Road-tested questions that help you uncover hidden needs that you can satisfy as you move through the sales process

Use creative strategies for addressing predictable customer problems in the sales process to create best practices, and then get that information in the hands of the people who can use it: your sales force.

There are many creative ways to deploy best practices. A large energy company we work with developed a go-to-market strategy focused on managing margin erosion and reducing price waterfall. They needed to make the right kinds of best practices data available to their army of sales representatives worldwide. First they tracked proprietary margin erosion and price waterfall data. Once they understood the metrics, they contracted with retired company executives who provided best practice processes and data insight. This best practice data was then distributed to their global sales team.

With this unique best practices sharing data, they were able to make dramatic improvements to their bottom line. A side benefit: sharing best practices and the ultimate success of the initiative led to stronger morale within the sales organization.

METRICS IN ACTION:
DATA THAT IMPROVES SALES PERFORMANCE

Having the data is one thing. Using it to improve sales performance is quite another. To that end, it's useful to distinguish between the data management uses to monitor progress, and the data the organization shares to motivate the right behavior of the sales team. We'll call them "dashboard" and "scoreboard" data.

Dashboard data is useful in that it helps you monitor progress as it happens and keep an eye on organizational performance. Dashboard data might include performance indicators by sales region, sales manager, and sales representative.

Scoreboard data reveals overall outcomes and results that can be used to track and share organizational performance, as well as motivate your sales team to improve its performance.

Dashboard data can also be transformed into scoreboard data. Here's how it works. Let's say you've determined that sales managers who have regular coaching sessions with their sales professionals get the best results from their teams. You would create a metric to measure how many times your sales managers have these coaching conversations. You would link that metric to the outcome of improved performance and set a standard for performance that you would then communicate to your sales force. Over time, you might see that managers who are less than 80 percent compliant with the standard are at the bottom of the heap in terms of performance.

At this point, you may choose to share this very valuable dashboard data with your sales organization in the form of scoreboard data. As soon as you report the information, your people (who are naturally competitive) will understand where they are in the pecking order and they will be motivated to compete with each other to improve. Making this information public can affect whether or not managers pay attention to what they truly need to do to attain optimal sales performance.

The trick is to decide what types of dashboard data you need to gather and analyze. Then you need to decide when, where, and with whom to share those findings in scoreboard form to motivate your sales team.

Summary

Closing the Gap: Data

- An organization can only evaluate and improve its performance by developing a deep understanding of the metrics that connect to achieving the company strategy at the customer interface. Savvy managers are able to pinpoint the precise metrics they need to measure to close the sales execution gap.

- To close the gap, discover what Pivotal Agreements advance the deal toward a profitable close.

- Track the data that matters: identify the metrics that connect to those Pivotal Agreements.

- Identify results metrics (which track how well you're carrying out your strategy) and process metrics (which track actions that lead to results) to measure results and predict future success.

- Improve performance by creating and using dashboard and scoreboard data to help you focus on areas that need improvement and motivate your sales team.

- Analyze your score and learn from it: assess the situation and diagnose the need to reengineer, fine-tune, and adjust your sales execution processes. Make the changes you need to make to improve your performance.

- Accelerate learning by sharing best practices with the entire sales organization.

5

DIALOGUE

*All the data in the world won't help unless it's used effectively
in critical dialogue with customers and within the sales team.*

We talk all the time. We talk about our numbers, our targets, our wins and
losses, our strategy, our golf games, our health.

We meet constantly to share and exchange information. There's the
annual meeting, the quarterly meetings, the monthly meetings, the weekly
meetings, the status meetings. Then there are the customer meetings:
the get-to-know-you meeting, the follow-up meeting, the follow-up to the
follow-up meeting, the meet-the-rest-of-the-decision-makers meeting,
the this-is-the-way-we-do-business meeting, the proposal meeting, the
closing meeting, and so forth. All that talking is important. Remember the
3D Model (fig. 5-1)? Dialogue—communication—is the second element.

We communicate constantly. So why is dialogue a critical component
of the last link?

Let me ask you this: Are your sales leaders having the *right* conversations with sales managers? Are they talking about strategy? Are they talking
about goals? Are they talking about standards of performance?

FIGURE 5-1   *The 3D Model: Dialogue*

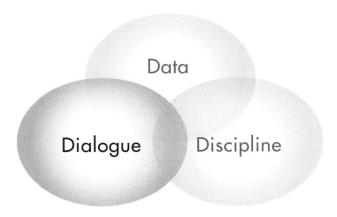

Are your sales managers having conversations with their salespeople that prompt the right behavior with customers? Are they translating your strategic initiatives into a specific game plan that reps can use in face-to-face conversations with customers? Are they modeling effective sales behavior and enforcing performance standards in every dialogue they engage in?

Are your salespeople having the right dialogue with their customers, using the right data to confirm their understanding of each customer's true needs? Are they using that understanding to sell solutions that create the greatest value for their customers?

They are? Are you sure?

With so many companies, from the Fortune 500 on down, failing to make their numbers on a regular basis, you've got to wonder.

THE POWER OF DIALOGUE

In great movies, there are lines of dialogue that become ingrained in our memories: "If you build it, they will come," "Go ahead, make my day," "Show me the money!" "I'll be back," "Round up the usual suspects . . ."

Why do you suppose those lines are so memorable? I think there are two reasons. First, the films laid the groundwork to ensure that audiences were fully in the moment, receptive, and deeply connected to what they were experiencing. Second, the characters speak the lines exactly right, at precisely the right times, and the dialogue, or in this case the lines, perfectly reflect some truth that leads to deeper understanding and insight. All of these phenomena cause the story to move forward in the right direction, toward the right result.

The best dialogue happens when the audience is ready to experience the impact of the line and the words perfectly encapsulate the intended message. Would you remember that moment in *Field of Dreams* when Kevin Costner walked out to survey his cornfield if the voice he heard had said, "Listen, kid, you've got a real opportunity here if you just build a baseball field"? Or how about Clint Eastwood snarling, "I think I have you where I want you and I'd really feel good if you'd do something stupid and give me an excuse to shoot you"? But if all the preparation is done well, a moment comes when all the conditions are right for the right words to have their full impact on the audience.

It works the same way in business, except the preparation and the critical conversations do not happen on a Hollywood set: they happen in offices during meetings with customers, and the dialogue is between a rep trying to orchestrate a successful sale and a customer.

High-performing sales professionals know that the outcome of a sale is heavily influenced by the precall preparation, timing, and quality of the dialogue the sales rep can engage in with the customer. Only the highest-quality dialogue on the right subjects yields the best results.

THE ULTIMATE DIALOGUE OPPORTUNITY: PIVOTAL AGREEMENTS

Pivotal Agreements are the ultimate dialogue opportunity. When sales organizations prepare their sales professionals to manage the dialogue that makes Pivotal Agreements, they dramatically increase the odds of winning larger and more profitable deals linked to their corporate strategy. If these agreements are handled poorly, the results are all too predictable: close rates, revenue volume, and margins will erode.

There are a lot of reasons why salespeople fail to make the most advantageous Pivotal Agreements. Here are a few I have encountered frequently over the years:

- The sales rep was unable to position the value of her company's product or service to his or her best advantage.
- The sales rep never fully understood the buyer's motivation or needs.
- The customer forced the price issue early on and the sales rep started discounting prematurely to win the business.
- The sales rep conceded without a plan and gave up too much.
- The customer made the best deal he could with the rep and then called the rep's boss, the EVP of sales, and negotiated an even better deal.

Sales organizations spend a lot of time and money trying to ensure that their representatives are positioned to have the right kinds of dialogues with their customers. But even if they know what agreements the sales reps need to make, they often don't zero in on the essential principles and practices that will allow the rep to have the kind of dialogue that produces the best results.

The key to structuring good dialogue is to plan. I have found that the most effective way to build a plan is to apply what I call the Dialogue Principles. These principles link strategy to sales methods and provide a structure for thinking through any important conversation you're going to have with a customer about the Pivotal Agreements that advance the sale.

STRUCTURING DIALOGUE USING THE DIALOGUE PRINCIPLES

When it comes to crafting optimal agreements, most sales organizations underperform. Ask executives about this and you'll hear a consistent message—that their people

- Focus on price too quickly and don't sell value

- Fail to understand underlying customer needs and don't create value as a result
- Make unnecessary concessions during the sales process, give away too much too quickly, and end up leaving money on the table

Habits like these undermine deal profitability and sabotage corporate strategy. You can improve your sales organization's ability to execute its agreements when you use and apply the Dialogue Principles to shape and focus your dialogue. These principles are simple and straightforward, but it's not always easy to get them right. They work within a two-part process.

The first part of the process involves creating value. You do that by managing information intentionally, identifying and satisfying underlying needs, and then positioning your solutions advantageously.

Once you create that value, you need to exploit it to get the best possible agreements by assessing and exerting your power, setting high targets, and exchanging value (fig. 5-2).

Let me frame each of these principles for you in the context of making good agreements.

VALUE CREATION

Building value is the process of demonstrating your product or solution's worth to the customer—an integral part of avoiding unnecessary

FIGURE 5-2   *The Dialogue Principles help you create value and execute agreements.*

The Dialogue Principles	
Value creation	• Manage information intentionally • Identify and satisfy underlying needs • Position your solutions advantageously
Agreement execution	• Assess and exert your power • Set high targets • Exchange value

discounting and protecting the organization's profit margin. You can create value for your product or service by managing information flow, understanding the customer's underlying needs, and positioning your solutions advantageously. Let's look at each of these principles in more depth.

Dialogue Principle: Manage Information Intentionally

Managing information intentionally means controlling the way you disclose information, and gathering information effectively. Many sales organizations believe that providing as much information as possible to the customer is a good selling practice that will work to the seller's advantage. Customers reinforce this belief by constantly asking for more information whenever a decision point is imminent. And after all, isn't giving customers what they want good selling? What's wrong with this tactic?

The problem is that there's no way to know how customers will use the information that you provide or what context they will use to evaluate the information. One thing you can be sure of is that if you provide customers with more information than they need to make an informed buying decision, the additional information will dilute your value and hurt the sale. In the worst case, the information could be used against you. Maybe your sales organization just gave the customer precisely the information he needs to undermine your bid and go with your competition.

This is why effective sales organizations plan in advance what information to share with the customer at each point in the sales process, with special attention to Pivotal Agreements. While they don't lie, mislead, or behave illegally or unethically, they don't share all the information they have at hand all the time. Only honest and accurate information is shared, and only when that sharing helps to position the solution better. This allows the salesperson to position the value of the company's solution as the conversation with the customer unfolds and the odds of making the right Pivotal Agreements increase.

How does dialogue support your sales organization's ability to manage information flow? First, understanding how to manage information heightens a sales rep's awareness that simply giving customers access to copious amounts of information won't move the sale forward. Second, understanding the specific information that creates value for the customer and your solution, as well as the information that creates no value, establishes a platform to guide the deal conversation.

When you anticipate customer expectations and reactions as part of the Sales Execution Plan, you will learn what information is required and what information is not required to move the sales process forward. Then you can make an intelligent decision about what information is appropriate to provide. That could mean that you supply the customer with the information he asked for, ask more questions, probe for deeper understanding, or give him the information he really needs as opposed to what he asked for, among other possibilities.

When it comes to gathering information, the more you get the better off you will be. There are many proven methods to gather it: you can ask open-ended questions, reframe the customer's questions and statements, probe for details, or acknowledge a question and defer answering until you gather more information.

When it comes to disclosing information, less is more. When it comes to gathering information, more is more. That is why you need forethought and planning to manage the information you give and receive. Your sales professionals need to think about what information they need and how they're going to get it. That means they must plan ahead and think about how they will answer questions without disclosing unnecessary information.

Dialogue Principle: Identify and Satisfy Underlying Needs

How many of your sales are torpedoed because your sales organization doesn't understand its customer's business needs until the final stages of contract negotiation—when it is too late?

Each constituency, at all levels of the customer organization, has different needs for your product or service to fill. Your sales organization needs to help its representatives focus on identifying those constituencies and determining what they need. Only through dialogue with your customers can you truly begin to understand their needs and how they will use your product or service to improve their own revenues and margins. When you have this information, you will be in a position to sell your full value and consummate a premium deal.

But here's the hitch. Customers and prospects often don't know what they need. They frame their requests for favors, information, and consideration in terms of wants. There is only one way to satisfy a want, and that is to give in. For example, your customer tells you he wants a lower price. There is only one way to satisfy that want—lower the price. The rep needs to probe for the underlying need instead.

Here's an example of an account executive who didn't probe for the underlying need when talking to a customer who knew what she wanted. Because the account executive didn't get at the underlying customer needs, he was not able to execute a sale that could have helped his company achieve their corporate strategy goals.

In the price-sensitive, commoditized environment of telecommunications, this company's strategy was to maintain margins. In this sales situation that meant the account exec needed to negotiate installation plans and scheduling to maximize efficiency and cost. It wasn't just performing on the job that was at stake, but also fulfilling commitments to existing clients.

When the account executive booked the sale and the service request made its way to scheduling, everyone jumped into high gear. Six hundred new lines were needed in six weeks at the customer's facility. The job was big. An installation schedule like this would require lots of resources that would cost plenty, but the installation was doable—if they pulled resources from other jobs. Was it worth it? Definitely. This client was big and it was getting bigger.

The telecommunications engineers pulled off the impossible, and the morning of the day of the big install eighteen trucks pulled up in front of the customer site just as the buyer sauntered into work. The account executive, on hand for the installation, approached his customer with pride. The customer looked aghast. "Why so many trucks?" she wondered. "We're here to do the install," he replied.

"But I only needed a few lines today . . . enough to get the receptionists up. The rest of the lines could have been staged over the next month and a half! We're not moving the whole crew out here all at once."

Oops! Not only were margins compromised, but the company lost money on the installation and lost a great deal of opportunity revenue from customers who had to be rescheduled.

Salespeople who probe and test to understand the customer's underlying needs rather than react to the stated want create a much greater opportunity to close better, more profitable sales. This principle allows the salesperson to sell the true value of his or her product or service while creating numerous ways to address the customer's needs.

By creating opportunities to engage the customer in the right kind of dialogue, you will create opportunities to uncover the needs behind the wants. And unlike the case with wants, there are usually many, many ways to satisfy a need.

Dialogue Principle: Position Your Solution Advantageously

Positioning your solution (or solutions) advantageously means framing the customer dialogue to increase the likelihood of gaining favorable Pivotal Agreements and optimal sales results.

No sales organization can achieve its goals if it fails to position its solution strategically. This means you must create context and frame your solution in a way that is advantageous to your organization and creates an emotional hook for the other party. You must know what the competition is up to, and create value in the minds of your buyers. You must understand and be able to articulate how your solution can help your customer improve her own revenue or margins.

Positioning your solution advantageously can result in a dramatic difference in your dialogues. A client that we work with makes and distributes large capital equipment used primarily for technology testing. Their state-of-the-art equipment requires the use of strong chemicals that cause degenerative changes to the equipment, so ongoing service is very important. If the equipment is not working properly (or at all), it can kill the productivity of the plant—to the tune of several hundred thousand dollars per hour. Thus, proper service and maintenance of the equipment is imperative.

This company's corporate strategy included improving sales size and deal profitability. Their objective was to get their customers to buy larger and higher margin business by selling a full solution (equipment, spare parts, and maintenance) rather than equipment only. To do this, they determined that one of the Pivotal Agreements they needed to make in their sales process was to get customers to accept a favorable cost/benefit analysis of service and equipment. If this agreement were made, larger and more profitable business would follow.

Knowing he needed to make that Pivotal Agreement to sell high-margin maintenance, a sales manager completed a Sales Execution Plan to get the best outcome. When it was time to talk to the buyer, he was prepared with a positioning theme and made the Pivotal Agreement. Here's how the meeting went:

The buyer positioned the negotiation something like this, "We know that you want to sell us a service contract, but we consider maintenance a cost. It's a cost to our P&L statement, and we expect you, if you really want to partner with us, to find ways to lower, not increase, our costs. And if your equipment is as good as you say it is, it shouldn't need much servicing anyway. Your company's responsibility is to provide a product to us that runs effectively and at a low cost point . . . and doesn't need a lot of service."

The sales executive listened carefully, but was well prepared to position the critical issue of the negotiation another way. He said, "The key issue for us to figure out is what level of productivity you want from your plant. We will work with you to determine the appropriate level of investment to achieve the desired level of productivity."

Using productivity of the plant as a positioning theme, the two became engaged in a lengthy dialogue about the best ways to achieve productivity levels. Ultimately, the buyer was persuaded that the productivity of the plant was critical to the total cost of ownership, which was more important than equipment price. Thus, effective positioning of the central issue—as productivity, not cost—enabled the parties to focus on the most appropriate issues and achieve a better result for both businesses.

Using a well-planned positioning theme can change the game and create high-value customer agreements.

AGREEMENT EXECUTION

Once you've built the value proposition, you can use the remaining Dialogue Principles to advance the sale toward your strategic goals and a profitable close. You do this by assessing and exerting your power, setting high targets, and exchanging value. Let's look at these principles in more detail.

Dialogue Principle: Assess and Exert Your Power

Power. We all have it. But do we all use it?

Assessing and exerting your power can lead to a better deal, as it did for one consumer electronics company. The electronic components sales representative had been engaged in a sales process with the new procurement manager of a large regional audiovisual chain for weeks, discussing the quarterly order size and inventory commitments the chain would make with her company. The procurement manager was holding fast to a small level of commitment at a lower-than-normal discounted price point.

The sales representative and her company had been doing business with this company for more than fifteen years, and over that time the sales rep had formed a number of excellent relationships at various levels of the organization. Frustrated, she called one of her senior-level contacts at the company and asked for coaching on how she should deal with the new manager's position and style. The senior-level manager quickly told the sales rep that this manager was under significant pressure to get the deal completed with her firm and get new inventory in the stores within the next thirty days.

Armed with this information, the next day the sales rep met with the procurement manager and politely told him that she was afraid that, because the two parties were so far apart in their discussions, they would not be able to reach a mutually satisfying agreement. She excused herself from the meeting and left the building. The sales rep didn't have to wait long for the call. Two days later the buyer called to report that they had decided to accept the sales rep's order size and inventory requests at the proposed discount levels. The value of the deal? More than nine hundred thousand dollars.

Sales personnel need to be able to assess and understand the power behind their relationships, their value, and their value proposition, and exert that power when it counts. It is critical to prepare your sales team to assess and exert their power in sales situations. When they are able to do this, it yields tremendous results and is intensely motivating.

Any sales organization can tap into one or all of its power components at any time. But first, it must know where its power lies. There is power in information: what you know about your customer base—their needs, their wants, their habits, and their business pressures—is a tremendous source of power. There is situational power: the ability to assess each situation, talk to the right people, get the right advice, and make the right moves are all sources of power. There is power in planning: thinking through the deal and identifying the Pivotal Agreements, trades, and negotiables is a source of enormous power. There is power in the organization: its reputation, its evenhandedness, its resources, its products, its services, and its support mechanisms. And finally, there is personal power: an individual who is prepared, who behaves with integrity, and who acts from conviction has significant power to move the deal in the right direction.

If you aren't engaging in dialogue that helps your sales professionals understand where their power is, they will not be able to assess it and exert it at the right moment.

A manufacturing company we have worked with sells its products through distributors. Because of the high-end nature of its products, its prices are often above the norm. Distributors often complained to the sales reps: "Your prices are too high. I can't make my margins if you can't give me a better discount. I'll have to stock my yard with your competitor's products."

Rather than cave in to their demands, the organization took a more creative and ultimately more fruitful approach. They assessed their power:

they had the best, most reliable products on the market (a fact validated by industry reports). And then they exerted their power: they launched an education campaign aimed at contractors, roofers, and end customers: "If you want the best, buy our products."

As the campaign unfolded they got the results they were looking for: the distributors' customers started to demand the manufacturer's product. Because the reps had exerted their power, they had a different conversation about discounts with distributors at subsequent deal discussions.

Dialogue Principle: Set High Targets

To make the best deals, you must follow the second principle of agreement execution: set high targets. Research shows that those who ask for more get more.

A company I know builds towers to create the network infrastructure for cell phone communications. This company—a leader in the industry—routinely built $100 million towers for telecom providers without ever asking for a down payment. In the spirit of asking for more, their sales organization determined that in future bid situations they would ask for a down payment. The first customer they approached using this tactic agreed, during the negotiation of a Pivotal Agreement early in the sales process, to give the tower manufacturer a $10 million down payment. If they hadn't set a target and asked, they would not have won the down payment.

Paradoxically, asking for more increases the perceived value of what you are selling. I worked with one account manager who set a high target that helped her build a better customer relationship and sell a significantly larger deal to the military. She set out to complete a Pivotal Agreement to get access to the base commander, which would help her close a large contract and execute one of her company's strategic goals—increasing dollars per contract.

The account manager was selling communications equipment to a major military base, for which security was a very important issue. Each year, the customer had a "Demo Day" and invited suppliers to provide products for display. Each year, the account manager's company chose to participate so they could continue doing business with the customer. However, by the time the company had its technical people set up and tear down its very elaborate communication system, they had spent many thousands of dollars in both money and time, and they had tied up costly products for the better part of two weeks.

Rather than just reflexively agreeing to participate in the Demo Day as the company had done in the past, in the spirit of setting high targets, the account manager said, "We would welcome the opportunity to participate, but in return we need to ask something from you. In order to provide the most value to your team and display the most powerful solution we can, we need a deep understanding of the strategic drivers relative to your communications needs for the base. Therefore, we would need an opportunity to interview the base commander and at least a couple of other key officers who help drive that strategy."

In the past, the sales account team had worked with a rather low-level communications buyer, who had little visibility to the base commander or involvement in the real communications strategy for the base. However, the rep persuaded the customer to arrange meetings with the top three base officers, and those meetings were most successful. The information the company gained enabled them to understand the range of business problems that they could help solve, and that enabled them to substantially improve both the demo they provided and the range of recommendations that they could make during the next contract negotiation.

By setting high targets and asking for more, the account manager was also able to add greater value to the relationship for both her company and the customer. Ultimately, the account manager more than doubled the sales volume with this key client, and she became a more strategic, trusted partner in the process.

If your sales organization is going to execute optimally, you must ensure that, in addition to setting high targets, your sales team identifies three points: their opening offer, their target, and when they will walk away.

Target, opening, and walk away—when these points are known and quantified, they give powerful shape to the deal management conversation that goes on between your sales organization and your prospects. And as I'll show you, a good concession strategy helps strengthen your opening and target offers during the sales process.

Sales organizations that execute optimally set high targets. When the customer balks or refuses, they test the boundaries within the customer's tolerance levels to find out the whys and wherefores behind that reaction. And, if need be, they're prepared to walk away from deals that aren't going to be profitable to the organization.

None of this can happen if you are not preparing your sales team to have good, well-thought-out dialogue with their customers around targets.

Dialogue Principle: Exchange Value

To execute optimal agreements, you need to exchange value—the final Dialogue Principle. When you have to make concessions in the sales process to advance the sale, it is critical to ask for something in return.

This principle has two parts: How you give things up is your concession strategy. Asking for something in return is called "making trades." You create value by exchanging value. Let's talk about these concepts one at a time.

Concession Strategy Invariably, sales professionals are going to be in dialogue with their customers and encounter pressure to concede on price, terms, delivery—some selling point. The request is often framed in this context: "Make the concessions and we can close the deal today. Don't make the concessions and I'll be forced to get back to your competitor."

Your sales team needs to be prepared for this moment by preplanning their concession strategy. With practice you'll find that a good concession strategy will ultimately help them achieve their target and opening offers.

There are several rules of thumb about the best way to concede:

- Concede slowly and with a plan. Giving too much too soon creates the wrong expectation on the customer's part.

- Make concessions incrementally smaller in the successive rounds of negotiation. The right concession pattern assures customers you've given as much as you can and they will be satisfied that they got the best deal they could.

- Only play "hardball"—refusing to make a concession under any circumstance—when you are not interested in maintaining a long-term relationship with your customer or in a one-time sale situation.

Conceding strategically involves not just giving things up the right way—but exchanging value in a way that optimizes the sale.

In some industries, particularly commoditized ones, salespeople are continually being asked to give things away. High-performing salespeople who use Sales Execution Plans will anticipate those requests and concede strategically in a manner that will allow them to ask for, and get, concessions that seed the next purchase.

Here's how one sales executive for a major communications firm handled concessions in a critical sales situation: "We were working on price concessions to roll over to the total solution. The CIO was making the decision and he prided himself on being a 'leading-edge' kind of guy. When he asked for the price break, we were ready. First, we acknowledged the importance of his request and asked if we could table it for the moment. We were able to defer the 'want' request while we asked a few questions to understand his total need so we could propose the optimal solution. We responded to some of the price pressure … but we also offered to outfit some of his building with a new wireless solution. He saw our move as a concession, we saw it as a way to deflect some of the price pressure and set up the next (wireless) deal."

Make Trades Many sales professionals look at a customer's requests to concede something to close the deal as a yes-or-no situation; therefore they don't think to ask for something back.

Value is subjective. Something that's worth a lot to you might not have much value to me. So how do you establish value? Two ways: initially by positioning, but as the deal advances toward close, you establish value through trades.

Most sales organizations know that to be successful they must create value and get their customer to pay for it. Yet as obvious as it might seem, many fail to realize that when they give something away to gain a key customer agreement, the giveaway has no value until something of value is exchanged in return.

I can't tell you how many sales organizations we've seen fail to create value for what they are selling, be it a product or service, because they concede to customer demands deep into the deal without getting enough in return—or worse, without getting anything in return. Little wonder that those companies regularly miss their numbers and fail to live up to Wall Street's expectations.

These marginal sales organizations don't understand that in order to create value, you must exchange—or trade—value. Why is that? Because exchanging value sets up a comparison in the customer's mind. He's thinking, "I'm trading this for that." That act of comparing things sets a relative value in the customer's mind to each item (or event) in the exchange.

- If the customer wants a lower price, trade value by asking for a higher volume commitment in return.

- If the customer wants a no-charge prototype to test the seller's solution, trade value by asking for a commitment to cover the costs of the prototype when and if they adopt the product.

- If the customer wants expedited delivery, trade value by asking for the shipment to include additional high-margin products.

When you give up something by asking for and getting something in return, you're teaching the buying organization how you want to be treated and you're establishing value at the same time.

Exchange value—make trades—in a methodical way. Know the primary and alternative, or elegant, negotiables you've got to exchange.

Negotiables are things you trade. Alternative, or elegant, negotiables are things you trade that have high value to the other party but low cost to you. Elegant negotiables work both ways. The elegant negotiable that you ask your customer for costs your client very little, but has high value to you.

A good elegant negotiable can sometimes look like an expensive concession, but as a client of ours proved, it can actually improve the profitability of the deal. One of their largest customers demanded that they place an on-site facilitator at the customer site to coordinate shipments. From the customer's perspective, this was a big deal and a gutsy request. From the company's perspective, it was a rare opportunity. They knew that if they negotiated the request the right way, they would be conceding something that was of high value to the customer, but saved them money. How does this trade save money? All shipments for that customer were coded manually, leaving the door open to inaccuracies. By "trading" an on-site facilitator using a computer coding unit for a price concession on the buyer's part, the company could work more accurately and faster, thus increasing the profitability of the deal.

This elegant negotiable resulted in another big win: it set a new competitive spec on the shipper's service product—that there be a person on-site provided by the shipper—that none of their competitors wanted to meet. In this situation, our client agreed to the buyer's request slowly and in return received a price concession. In the end, this agreement was very favorable for both parties.

Another organization we worked with—a leading-edge technology company—used indirect financing as an alternative negotiable to defray price pressure and close a huge deal with one of the largest retailers in the world. Here's how the lead negotiator told the story: "We got a $20 million deal eight months earlier based on offering a financing solution. It's not unusual for a customer to say the price is too high. We came to find out that it's not about our price being too high. It's a cash flow/budget problem that our customer had that could be solved by financing the payment terms, which we did."

THE COUNTERINTUITIVE NUANCES OF DIALOGUE

The Dialogue Principles are straightforward and logical. They form an integral part of beating profit killers and executing the company strategy. But applying them in dialogue with customers often runs against intuition for sales professionals.

For example, customers often want to focus immediately on price. It is counterintuitive to acknowledge this request and then defer the discussion while you probe for more information that creates the opportunity for you to expand buying criteria and sell your overall value proposition. Deferring a customer request creates tension. Asking for a trade might also be tension producing, and again it is a counterintuitive act. Exerting your power also creates the possibility for tension in your customer relationships.

There is no denying that there is stress and tension when you're in that zone between looking out for your own self-interest and giving the customers what they want. And tension can be uncomfortable—something we all want to avoid. However, with practice using the Dialogue Principles, you will find that you can use this tension to get a more advantageous agreement.

When you're in a tense situation, your intuitive reaction is to give in to reduce tension. The counterintuitive reaction is to stay in the tension and work through it. When you do this, you often come out with a better solution. By the way, staying in the tension in a sales situation is much easier when you have a thoroughly thought-out Sales Execution Plan guiding you.

The sales rep for a large shipping company found himself in a tense situation when his customer demanded that their shipments be picked up daily at 2:30 PM, when they closed for business. The shipper did not want to have to make that concession because it meant scheduling a special pickup, which would wreck havoc with established routes and would greatly increase the shipper's cost of servicing this customer's business.

They worked out all the details of their agreement, except this one. Days went by as the tension rose higher and higher. But the sales rep decided to hold the tension and stick with his plan. In the end this strategy paid off. The customer and the shipping company worked together to find a reasonable solution and finally they reached an agreement. The shipper built a lockbox on the customer's loading dock. The packages were safe; people could go home; and the shipper could make the pickup much later in the day during one of its regularly scheduled routes. Staying with the tension created a great solution.

Because applying the Dialogue Principles is sometimes counterintuitive, sales professionals need to continually be reminded to use them. Sales organizations can do this by making sure the right dialogue is happening between sales managers and sales representatives and between sales leadership and management. I'll have more to say about this in the next chapter on discipline—it takes discipline to ensure the right conversations are happening within the sales organization so that the right dialogue can occur between the sales professional and the customer.

Summary

Closing the Gap: Dialogue

- The right dialogue will help you move the needles on the metrics that lead to achieving your corporate strategy.

- Take advantage of the ultimate dialogue opportunity by identifying and making the Pivotal Agreements you need to advance the sale to a profitable close.

- Prepare your sales team to have the right kinds of dialogue with your customers to make Pivotal Agreements by ensuring they know and use the Dialogue Principles. Create value by managing information flow, identifying and satisfying underlying needs, and positioning your solutions advantageously. Execute agreements by assessing and exerting your power, setting high targets, and exchanging value through concessions and trades.

- Managers should seize the opportunity to have regular deal management conversations with sales professionals so their sales reps are properly prepared to have the right kind of dialogue with their customers.

6

<u>DISCIPLINE</u>

It's not enough to have the right data and the right dialogue;
to make things happen, you need discipline.

Instilling discipline throughout your sales organization is the final and
perhaps most important element of the 3D Model (fig. 6-1). The cost of
failing to do it right is high. As one sales executive reported to me recently,
"In our world, the phone rings and, suddenly, you are into it . . . without
the discipline, people start winging it . . . there's just too much at stake . . .
with margins as tight as they've been, a 1- to 2-cent premium can be the
difference between making money and losing money."

Chances are, the stakes are high in your industry as well, and you have a
sense of urgency about introducing the right disciplines to carry out your
strategy at the point of customer contact.

I say *right disciplines* because you haven't reached this stage in your
career without some discipline in your life. And chances are you already
have elements of discipline built into your sales organization. For example,
most companies have a disciplined approach to expense reporting and
reimbursement. They periodically review deals in their pipeline; they have

FIGURE 6-1   *The 3D Model: Discipline*

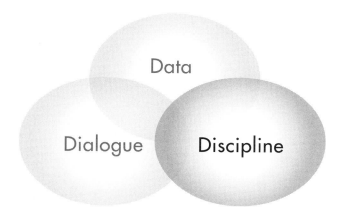

regular weekly or monthly meetings with their sales team; and they require their salespeople to report on the status of deals, share information about competitors, and talk about various mission-critical factors.

So, many sales executives think they've got discipline—and they do—but they don't always have the right disciplines in place when it comes to making the strategy work at the customer interface.

Here's how it goes in a lot of organizations: The senior sales executive articulates a sales strategy that reinforces the corporate strategy and assumes that everyone knows what to do. Then he or she moves on to the next initiative. Sales professionals who value speed over planning act as lone rangers and move toward closing the deals they can rather than planning and executing the deals they should. Sales management supports this behavior because they are busy putting out fires and don't implement critical coaching, so they are unable to monitor the effects of their decisions and actions and those of their salespeople. In an effort to close business as fast as possible, sales managers are directive and make concessions without thinking about or understanding the consequences of what they are doing. Under pressure from sales and sales management to pass nonstandard deals through quickly because "so much revenue is at stake," deal approvers do not require appropriate deal planning and background information to ensure the best possible revenue and margins, and reluctantly accept another unprofitable deal.

In this chapter, you'll learn to leverage the discipline processes you already have in place to help you make discipline a profitable reality.

WHY ORGANIZATIONS DODGE THE DISCIPLINE DICTUM

The word *discipline* can evoke unpleasant images. "I'm going to discipline you for this breach of conduct." Wham! A sharp word, a firm hand, a privilege withdrawn. Punishment—leading to banishment, humiliation, anger, fear, perhaps even hatred. Most people see discipline as negative. Perhaps that's why so few organizations emphasize discipline as a value.

But discipline is a critical component of the 3D Model. When you run a disciplined organization, you create a framework within which your employees can act and react to advance the sales process. Discipline produces a safety net, because the norms, standards, and rules are known. No one has to waste time and energy second-guessing the strategy, the tactics, or any other basic assumptions about roles or expectations. You eliminate the doubt and uncertainty that plagues so many companies and free your sales organization to focus their best and most creative energy where it belongs: on crafting and closing deals.

This kind of discipline is especially critical in light of survey findings presented in the July 2006 *McKinsey Quarterly*, in which managers from all main regions and sectors acknowledged the increasing significance of speed and agility required to improve competitive edge. In the quest to achieve greater speed and agility, McKinsey reports, "many are grappling with a wide range of organizational, behavioral and attitudinal barriers—notably those that hamper quick decision making and clear accountability."[1] Embedding the right disciplines, especially those focused on the principles I emphasize throughout this book, speeds up decision making and hard-wires accountability into the organization. But speed is not the only benefit of discipline.

The highest-performing sales organizations are those that are clear about the requirements for creating revenue and optimizing margins, and consciously embed and reinforce sales and deal management methods that focus on the key agreements for success. These organizations not only embrace discipline as a value, they put the necessary structures and processes into place so that discipline becomes an operational norm.

Yet not every company chooses to or is able to instill such organizational discipline, and you've got to wonder why. One CEO I've worked with over the years who has skillfully instilled discipline up and down his organization put it simply: "It boils down to a tolerance for bad behavior."

Let's face it: the operative norm in a lot of companies is tolerance for mediocrity. When things get hard, when people push back, we take the path of least resistance. If somebody doesn't want to do something, we simply tolerate it. And unfortunately a lot of companies don't have checks and balances in place to remedy this.

Not long ago, I attended a meeting with senior executives in a client company where I watched as the division head of this company declined to adopt a mandated methodology that was a proven success in other divisions (with a quantified revenue lift and shorter sales cycle time as a result of implementing the process). After that, the EVP of sales was disinclined to push further. Without discipline, the company lost its edge and failed to make its numbers that quarter or any other quarter in the near term.

I suggest that you scrutinize your organization's behavior and ask yourself, Are we using a proven strategy execution process that focuses us on making the Pivotal Agreements we need to optimize revenue and margins in each and every sales situation? And are we truly committed to requiring compliance with the process?

I'm going to give you a lens to view this concept through so you can get your organization disciplined in its strategy execution.

THE ELEMENTS OF DISCIPLINE

I've learned from experience that when a sales organization positions itself to carry out its corporate strategy by equipping its sales team with discipline, it can optimize revenue, margins, and shareholder value. The key elements of discipline are

- A structured Sales Execution Plan
- A focus on obtaining Pivotal Agreements connected to financial metrics, using data and dialogue to achieve your sales strategy goals
- Use of the Dialogue Principles and related best practices
- Deployment through existing sales management processes and systems
- Sponsorship from senior executives and the sales leadership team
- Reinforcement and measurement from management

This simple, powerful discipline for account management and review must be introduced and then reinforced through repeated, mandatory application. Let's look at each of its elements in detail (fig. 6-2).

The Sales Execution Plan

The Sales Execution Plan is a written document that defines an organization's specific plans for executing corporate strategy at the point of customer interface. Creating a plan and sticking to it makes for huge payoffs. As one client put it, "The guy who has engaged in the most pre-work usually wins."

Make the Planning Process Simple so that People Will Use It I once worked with a client who had a convoluted seventeen-step planning process in place. It was overengineered and so complex that nobody used it. At one critical juncture, this is what happened instead: An area sales manager who had been asked to parachute in on the deal flew in the night before the key negotiation. The next morning the sales team planned their strategy for the key negotiation over breakfast and took notes on a napkin. Because they lacked a planning discipline, and were not sufficiently prepared, the buyer caught them off guard. They made unnecessary commitments by giving poor answers to questions they hadn't anticipated. They allowed the customer to establish the agreement playing field with more focus on price

FIGURE 6-2   *Key elements of strategy execution discipline*

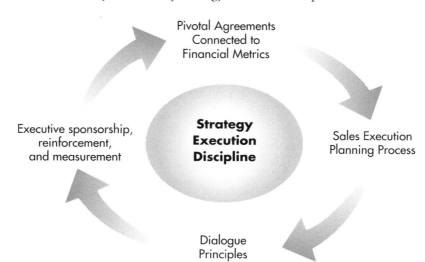

than value. The team lacked a cohesive plan and was not aligned around a common execution strategy. As a result, they left millions of dollars of margin on the table.

Use the Plan to Save Time This idea might seem counterintuitive; after all, planning takes time, so how can it save time? Our research has shown that good, comprehensive sales execution planning shortens sales cycle time by an average of 20 percent. This is largely due to the fact that good planning results in fewer deal approval iterations before an approval decision is made.

Use the Plan to Coach all the Players Sales managers can use the plan to coach their sales reps on how to do things right. And the entire sales team can use the plan as the foundation from which they communicate deal status and strategy to any team members that engage in the sales process at different points in the sales cycle.

Deal Planning Meetings Should Focus Everyone on Having the Right Dialogue
"Let's look at the plan. How have we positioned our solution? What

strategic needs does our solution help our customer solve? What agreements have we made? What Pivotal Agreements do we still need to make? What are our targets? What is our concession strategy? What have we already traded? Are there additional trades we can make to enhance our margins and add greater value to our solutions?"

Make the Plan Specific to What You Are Selling Remember that while the plan has standard elements, organizations cannot take a cookie-cutter approach to their planning process. Plans are different for each organization and yours must be specific to what you are selling.

Use the Plan to Enforce Discipline in Deal Escalation and Exception Approval This will help you embed a process that provides better data to the deal approvers, which they can use in turn to make better decisions, faster.

When you use a structured Sales Execution Plan, you will ensure that everyone in your sales organization is working on the same page. No more winging the precall strategy meeting at the local coffee shop just prior to meeting with the customer. Engaging in structured sales execution planning gets people marching in rhythm toward the goal of optimizing revenue and margins.

Focusing on Pivotal Agreements

When you embed the discipline of identifying and planning how to make Pivotal Agreements, you can be sure your salespeople are focusing their efforts on the critical components that will lead to the best deal possible.

Here's how one company leveraged dialogue and discipline within their sales organization and with their customers. A medical supply company determined that one Pivotal Agreement they needed was to actually meet with the doctors who could prescribe their product to patients. When they had "quality face time" with the doctor, they were often able to secure a buy decision—thus furthering their corporate strategy of increasing the size of their customer relationships.

While this company's reps were excellent at providing data about their products, including technical information on their product's efficiency, it took too much time to convey the information to busy, preoccupied doctors. The sales organization realized that they needed to craft a winning dialogue that was very short—anywhere from thirty seconds to two minutes—that communicated the essential information and positioned their product advantageously. The solution—conceived in dialogue sessions within the sales organization—was to formulate a disciplined approach through sales execution planning and make sure reps were fully prepared to take advantage of their fleeting opportunities for dialogue with the doctors.

The right data can also be extremely useful when you need to make Pivotal Agreements. One of our clients successfully integrated data into helping reps achieve an important go-to-market goal: getting their customers to switch to a new contracting model that rewarded their best customers rather than treating all of them equally.

One key to making the initiative successful was putting data about the buying history of their customers and market data on buying patterns of their customer's customers (based on point-of-sale research from scanners and other sources) in the hands of the salespeople. The data provided the content for high-gain customer dialogue—the likely sales volume the customer should sign up for in the new contract.

Using the Dialogue Principles and Related Best Practices

In their Sales Execution Plans, sales professionals need to specify how they will apply the Dialogue Principles (fig. 6-3) introduced in the last chapter. Salespeople can use these principles to help them flesh out their plans for how they will create value and secure each agreement that advances the sale toward a profitable close. This requires the discipline to ask themselves a series of questions and then write down the answers. The questions might sound like these: *What is my plan for managing information? What techniques can I use to get at my customer's underlying needs? What's the best way to position my solution? What opening offer should I make to hit my target? At what point should I walk away? What trades can I make that have high value and low cost? What best practices can I tap into to help me execute a better sale? What is my concession strategy?*

FIGURE 6-3 *The Dialogue Principles inform the planning process.*

The Dialogue Principles	
Value creation	• Manage information intentionally • Identify and satisfy underlying needs • Position your solution advantageously
Agreement execution	• Assess and exert your power • Set high targets • Exchange value

A global energy company estimated that they were losing $50 million a year because their clients were not complying with payment terms. The controller told us, "Payment terms and payment beyond terms are significant to our working capital. There is a lot of money that gets left on the table and it is worth going after. If we were just paid on time, it would be worth about $50 million to our bottom line each year." Analysis of the data revealed that the company's profit margins were eroding at a rate of approximately two hundred thousand dollars a day, and that was having a serious impact on cash flow.

To support their corporate strategy of improving the percentage of payments received on time, they formulated a sales strategy around getting a Pivotal Agreement on client payment terms. By employing two key Dialogue Principles—planning out their targets and having a concession strategy, then executing their plan during the Pivotal Agreement–making process—sales professionals were able to "stop the leak."

Deployment Through Existing Processes and Systems
Discipline is deployed through sales management processes and systems that most companies already have in place, such as

- One-on-one coaching sessions
- Team meetings
- Deal escalation processes
- CRM systems (pipeline review and/or projections)

Use the coaching opportunity that arises between sales managers and sales representatives. Use the opportunity that arises at weekly sales meetings to share best practices. Use monthly and quarterly meetings to communicate details about the strategy, how it's supposed to work, and what kind of results you're getting. Use the annual meeting to communicate the vision, and then reinforce the message all year long.

Here's how deploying discipline through existing sales management processes and systems can work: At a consumer products company, the strategic goal was margin improvement. Sales management identified the Pivotal Agreements they needed to make to improve margins. They used their regular management meetings to deploy the initiative. At the launch meeting they introduced their sales professionals to the Pivotal Agreements that my firm helped them identify. Then they introduced a new concept they called "the margin conversation."

The margin conversation went something like this: "What should happen whenever a Pivotal Agreement on a deal of a certain magnitude presents itself as part of a customer engagement process? What should happen between sales managers and sales representatives so that they can execute that agreement in a way that maximizes margins?"

Sales professionals turned to the Dialogue Principles and asked themselves, "How can we apply the principles to achieve the best agreements?" For example, "In this situation, what are the Pivotal Agreements? What is our target? How do we open? When do we walk away? How will I get at the customer's underlying needs? How can I address those needs using creative alternative negotiables? What trades can I make to get a favorable Pivotal Agreement?"

The margin conversation put the onus on the salespeople to work on the right things in preparation for their regularly scheduled meetings with their managers. Sales reps prepared for the margin conversation with their managers by creating a simple but thorough Sales Execution Plan. This planning helped them think through their execution strategy (using the Dialogue Principles) and created an important product: a document they could review with the manager. This became especially important for larger, more complex agreements.

The importance of having the margin conversation was and is reinforced at regular monthly sales team meetings. Sales managers lead discussions of best practices for using the Dialogue Principles to consummate more favorable agreements leading to better deals with their customers.

Sponsorship from the Top Leadership

I have often said that selling is a team sport, and it's true. I think the effort to execute corporate strategy in sales is analogous to the game of basketball.

As Malcolm Gladwell writes in his best-selling book *Blink*: "Basketball is an intricate, high-speed game filled with split-second, spontaneous decisions."[2] Doesn't that describe what it's like to be on the front line, face-to-face with a customer, knowing you've got to deliver? Strategy is critical—planning offensive and defensive match-ups and plays that will take advantage of your team's given strengths and the opposition's weaknesses. But when you're on the court it's all about executing the plan effectively through rehearsed spontaneity.

Gladwell goes on to say, "But that spontaneity is possible only when everyone first engages in hours of highly repetitive and structured practice—perfecting their shooting, dribbling, and passing and running plays over and over again—and agrees to play a carefully defined role on the court. How good people's decisions are under fast-moving, high-stress conditions of rapid cognition is a function of training and rules and rehearsal."[3] You achieve excellence under this kind of pressure in selling by adhering to a disciplined approach.

A lot of people are involved in making a deal. There are those who create the strategy, those who communicate the strategy, those who execute the strategy, those who measure compliance with the corporate strategy . . . and the list goes on. The efforts of all those people must ultimately be coordinated—through discipline—if the organization expects to execute strategy optimally.

Discipline starts at the top. It must be articulated and modeled inside the executive suite first in order for it to become a critical daily practice that the entire sales organization follows. Top sales executives and the leadership team must elicit disciplined behavior from deal makers, their managers, and sales support staff.

Reinforcement and Measurement from Management

When management reinforces discipline and measures whether or not salespeople are meeting the standards, they influence behavior and get better deals made. Chalk it up to the Hawthorne effect: work-group norms affect productivity. If you set the norms, the productivity will improve.

An integral part of reinforcement involves holding people accountable. Everyone responsible for planning sales and negotiating profitable deals with customers to meet management's strategic goals needs to be held accountable for the way they conduct business. They need to restructure their daily activities so they can use discipline in key deals. You can make people accountable when you coach them the right way. This means holding yourself back from solving their problems and coaching them to solve their own problems.

Another reinforcement tool is measurement. Using the results and process metrics I introduced in chapter 5, you can measure performance. When you know where you need to concentrate to reach your strategic goals, you can transform your dashboard data into scoreboard data and use it to motivate your sales force.

Once you embed discipline into your sales organization, it will become such an integral part of the way you do business that people won't even talk about deals outside the framework I've outlined in this book. They won't want to waste their time on any other type of conversation, and rightly so. To get sustained results, you have to continually practice using the process and make disciplined deal management habitual.

FOUR DISCIPLINE TIPS THAT LEAD TO BIG WINS

1. Start with a Thorough Analysis of Your Pivotal Agreements

Disciplined sales organizations analyze their sales processes and identify, in advance, all the Pivotal Agreements they need to make to create the conditions that lead to a profitable close.

A major financial services company sells its products through brokers and other intermediaries. In order for the final contract to be profitable, the salesperson is required to identify and successfully make a series of

Pivotal Agreements throughout the sales process. Here is a list of some of those agreements:

- Getting enough information or the right information from brokers to be able to craft the right solution
- Working through brokers to gain access to the "real" decision makers in the sales process when necessary
- Getting clients to look at the services the company can bring to the table and not just at price
- Managing broker expectations around critical process issues (billing, payments, etc.)
- Being able to build and maintain a good relationship while still saying *no*
- Building internal agreements with underwriting, billing, and contracting to enable profitable agreements with brokers

2. Get Managers Excited About Discipline First

Early involvement will give sales managers faith in the importance of discipline (fig. 6-4). They will then have the motivation to get their people involved in planning, using data, and having the right kinds of dialogue.

3. Embed Discipline into the Process of Approving Exception Deals

Effective organizations embed discipline into the process for approving exceptional off–price list deals.

At a global test and measurement equipment company, the sales strategy was geared toward achieving a primary goal: reduce discounting by 10 percent. The solution: prepare the sales team to have the right kind of dialogue with customers, and ensure the team complies by asking them to complete the Sales Execution Plan when they ask for authority for exceptional pricing. The salesperson is held accountable for showing how he or she will execute his or her Pivotal Agreements around pricing at the lowest possible discount. The Sales Execution Plan is part of a required deal escalation form: it is the tool that communicates the parameters of the deal to the product managers who approve or reject the request.

FIGURE 6-4 *Deploying the discipline*

Why Managers Need to "Get It" First

---

1. Communicates to the rest of the sales organization
   - "We're committed to getting results."
   - "We're holding you accountable for results using this methodology."
   - "You have a unique and important role in the initiative."
2. Provides opportunities for managers to hear messages directly from executives in a group
3. Orients them to live their role before roll-out
4. Allows managers to
   - Integrate content into their own daily work and have early successes
   - Understand and buy in to their coaching role with their reps
   - Presell the approach to their sales team
   - Assume their leadership role as the new discipline approach is rolled out
5. Gets managers excited about the discipline on a gut level
6. Early successes create internal buzz and momentum before sales rep roll-out

---

Sales leaders would do well to insist on sales execution planning documentation before getting involved in escalated sales. Take these "moment of truth" opportunities, when your salespeople are watching to see if you're serious about discipline, to ask for the plan.

4. Insist on Disciplined Use of the Sales Execution Plan by the Entire Sales Team Throughout the Sales Process

An international shipping company was going after more business at better terms with an existing client, a leading technology firm renowned for its negotiation prowess. Throughout their long, difficult, and protracted sales process, the sales team used its execution plan with discipline. The team leader made sure that the plan was updated on a regular basis and that the dozen or so members of the sales team shared information constantly. In fact, the plan was updated more than ten times in order to ensure that everyone was on the same page regarding the needs of all parties, targets, positioning, concession strategy, and so forth.

The customer team tested the sales team's mettle on many occasions: refusing to talk, making inappropriate demands, walking away. But the selling team, by relying on their Sales Execution Plan, was able to stay on track and respond from strength and knowledge rather than emotion. The planning discipline and diligence paid off. After extremely difficult negotiations that lasted many months, they made a deal that represented millions of dollars of committed business, including a joint product/solution launch.

After the deal was consummated, the CEO of the buying company called the CEO of the selling company to congratulate him on creating the right opportunity to move ahead on a far more strategic relationship. Planning works!

FIGURE 6-5 *Quick tips for implementing successful discipline*

- Communicate clearly.
- Reinforce accountability.
- Let the Pivotal Agreements in your sales cycle drive the planning process.
- Focus your sales team on planning: require the use of a Sales Execution Plan and make sure everyone who touches the deal knows the plan.
- Motivate people to develop good habits through the disciplined use of scoreboard data.

Summary

Closing the Gap: Discipline

- Discipline is an essential part of executing corporate strategy at the point of customer interaction.

- The key elements of discipline are
  - o A structured Sales Execution Plan
  - o A focus on obtaining Pivotal Agreements connected to financial metrics, using data and dialogue to achieve your sales strategy goals
  - o Use of the Dialogue Principles and related best practices
  - o Deployment through existing sales management processes and systems
  - o Sponsorship from senior executives and the sales leadership team
  - o Reinforcement and measurement from management

THE UNBREAKABLE CHAIN

7

LINKING IT TOGETHER

For a strategy to succeed,
every player must know and execute his or her role.

If you're going to close the gap between your corporate strategy and the results you need, you've got to be able to execute your strategy successfully. Until everyone in your sales organization can consistently and proactively employ the power of the 3D Model—data, dialogue, and discipline—to obtain the Pivotal Agreements in each deal they are working on, you will not be able to achieve your goals at the point of customer interface. Instead, you will find yourself reacting too often to competitor moves, customer demands, and internal organizational roadblocks.

IF THIS WERE EASY EVERYONE WOULD BE DOING IT

Let's say you've got a legal problem. What do you do? Call up your chief legal counsel and get him on the case. Let's say you want to launch an advertising campaign. No problem. Transfer the responsibility of putting together a powerful campaign to your EVP of marketing. Let's say there's a new piece of software out there that is mission critical to the success of your organization. Your CIO is the logical person to bring it into the organization.

Now, let's say you're not achieving the goals of your corporate strategy. If you're the CEO or EVP of sales, who do you call for help? Is there one group that can help you solve the problem? Would it be strategic planning, corporate development, sales, marketing, manufacturing, administration, training, the information technology group? If you are a sales leader and your organization is not making its numbers, what do you do and who do you call for help? Your sales executives, sales managers, your EVP? It could be any or all of the above—because executing the corporate strategy at the customer interface cuts across all lines of your organization.

Strategy execution can't be delegated to one department head. Carrying out a comprehensive, multifaceted corporate strategy requires the energy, thoughts, and commitment of lots of people. To execute sales well, you must build into your organization a discipline and a mentality that focuses on excellence in applying strategy. It's not easy. If it were easy everyone would be doing it.

So where do you start? By closing the escape hatches.

SECURE THE ESCAPE HATCHES

You've heard of escape hatches. Think submarine. When you're at the dock loading supplies and personnel, you want the hatches open. When you're submerged and on course to fulfill the mission, you want them locked down tight because you know it only takes one leak to sink the boat.

The same dynamic exists in sales organizations. Unless you secure all the escape hatches you will not be able to execute a profitable corporate strategy. Unfortunately, in the majority of sales organizations, people look for escape hatches all the time—taking the easy way out, passing responsibility to someone else instead of holding themselves accountable. To make matters worse, leaders are often distracted by the daily grind of working in a highly competitive environment where pressure is intense and the demands of the marketplace are constantly shifting. As a consequence, they don't even notice that time, effort, and money are seeping through open escape hatches.

We recently worked with a global company that invested millions of dollars (and countless hours of staff time) implementing a deal-tracking system to ensure that all requests for deal exceptions were handled quickly and profitably. The goal? Decrease the cycle time between pricing requests and closed contracts, and allow fewer costly price concessions.

Several months after the system was up and running, we interviewed all the key managers in the company's sales organization who were tasked with managing the new system. We made a striking discovery: every key manager had a reason why he or she felt exempt from enforcing use of the new deal tracking system. They justified their behavior in various ways (fig. 7-1), but everyone had an escape hatch that allowed him or her to avoid doing the right things. And unfortunately management lacked the discipline to enforce compliance, close the escape hatches, and insist that all the key players actually use the system to process their exception deals. Needless to say, the sales initiative failed within twelve months. Sales went flat, margin goals were not met, the board of directors put more pressure on the CEO, and the stock price continued to fall.

Unfortunately this scenario plays out in many major corporations today. Somebody comes up with a viable way to improve things, and the organization spends a great deal of time and money creating the infrastructure to make it happen. But at the moment of truth—when management needs to hold people accountable for meeting the new standards—they back off. The result: people shirk their commitments and fall back into comfortable, familiar ways of doing things.

This cycle sends the wrong message. It reinforces people's belief that if they ignore the initiative, it will go away.

For the senior executive, a prerequisite for optimally executing corporate strategy at the point of customer interaction is to secure the hatches. Once those escape hatches are closed and people know you are serious, they will listen.

FIGURE 7-1 *Typical "escape hatches"*

The Player	The Justification
Sales professionals	"Don't confuse me with another system. My job is to close sales and keep my customers happy. Just leave me alone and let me do my deals. Let me see if I can find a way to work around the new system so I can focus on what's really important."
Sales managers	"I don't have time for this! I put out fires all day long. If I've got to comply with one more system I'm going to scream. Hey, I understand that management needs to control price concessions, but I don't have time to deal with all the paperwork; I've got reports due at the end of the month and I'm giving a presentation at the next management meeting. Let me see if I can find a way to get my exceptional pricing the old way instead of by using the new system."
Deal approvers	"I understand that management wants us to use the new system, but as far as I'm concerned this is just another way for them to micromanage my work. I'm paid to move the deals through the system, not slow them down with layers of bureaucratic process. This is the deal approval department, not the deal avoidance department. Let me see if I can make it look like I'm using the system without putting the time into it."
Sales leadership	"I know they don't like the new system. And I know the pressure everyone is under to hit the numbers. I think we'll be flexible in implementing it for a while. If the troops work around the system by getting deals approved through back channels, that'll be OK, as long as we hit our numbers."

Once you've got their attention, explain their roles in the corporate strategy and the consequences of nonperformance.

THE SELLING ORGANIZATION: EVERYONE HAS A ROLE TO PLAY

The single most important factor in determining whether an enterprise's strategy will succeed at the point of the customer interface is not its people's compensation, training, or product knowledge. The most important factor is making the sales task clear: ensuring that salespeople know exactly what is expected of them; making sure they have the right tools, information, and processes in place to succeed; and having the right reinforcement and compliance structure in place.

Getting your sales organization firing on all cylinders starts with making sure everyone understands what he or she needs to do. Roles need to be defined, and the people filling them need to understand their parts. Only then can you take the next step: building true accountability for strategy execution at all levels in the organization.

In the classic selling organization there is a hierarchy of leaders, salespeople, and staff that supports the sales process before, during, and after the deal is made and the contract is signed. In disciplined, high-performing sales organizations, all the players at all levels in the sales organization act in unison. They understand the mission, the strategy, and their role in executing the strategy to achieve the desired results. Each engages in his or her own processes, taps in to key information, and communicates in ways that support the execution of the corporate strategy at the point of customer contact.

Savvy sales leaders understand who needs to do what and make sure every player on their sales teams knows the following:

- His or her unique role in the process
- The consequences for the team if that role is not executed
- The sales execution methods necessary to be successful in the deal-making arena
- How his or her performance will be tracked

Although every organization is unique, in our experience there are generally six distinct kinds of players who influence how strategy fares at the point of customer interface: the CEO, the top sales executive, the deal approvers, the sales managers, the sales reps, and the sales/customer support team.

Each player has a unique role. If he or she fails to perform that role optimally, there are consequences for the strategy (fig. 7-2). For the purposes of

this discussion, I'll take a top-down approach and describe these roles and
the consequences of not performing, and then give you a checklist for each
player in your organization.

The CEO

In a great selling organization, the CEO sets and articulates the corporate
strategy for customer interaction and is committed to applying it. The
CEO is so committed that he or she insists on reviewing Sales Execution

FIGURE 7-2   *The high-risk consequences of less than optimal role
execution are real.*

Player	Unique Role in Sales Execution Plan	Consequences of Not Performing
Chief executive officer	Sets and articulates corporate strategy and commits to execution	The gap between strategy and results persists and revenue and margin are not optimized.
Senior sales executives	Own and manage execution of the corporate strategy at the customer interface through positioning and modeling high-performing strategy execution behavior	Sales managers conclude that leadership gives "lip service" to corporate strategy execution but tolerates mediocrity when it comes to implementation.
Deal approvers	Act as strategic gatekeepers	Deals don't meet "good sale" criteria.
Sales managers	Coach rather than direct sales professionals; reinforce the use of the Sales Execution Plan focused on making Pivotal Agreements	Sales representatives fall back into intuitive and unprofitable selling.
Sales professionals	Execute sales by making Pivotal Agreements using the Dialogue Principles	The company experiences sub-optimal revenue growth, account profitability, and customer satisfaction.
Sales/customer support team	Provides data and support, as well as customer follow-up	Margins decrease during and after the sale.

Plans prior to any meetings with customers in which he or she participates. When the CEO doesn't "walk the talk," others in the organization will conclude that senior management is not paying attention and that executing the strategy isn't really that important.

I've got a lot more to say about the role of top management in the next chapter. But in this chapter, I want to make it crystal clear what the rest of the selling organization has to do to fulfill their part in executing the corporate strategy effectively.

Senior Sales Executives

In an execution-oriented sales organization, the top sales executive (often with the help of a sales operations group) breaks down the customer interface segment of the company strategy into actionable and measurable events, embeds the 3D Model to achieve the desired results, and then holds the team accountable for following through with the process.

To do this, top sales executives must take responsibility for and manage the execution of the corporate strategy at the customer interface. They must position their sales organization to achieve the sales strategy goals and model high-performing strategic behavior at every opportunity—which includes reviewing all Sales Execution Plans before meeting with customers. They must also request periodic strategy execution updates, including specific examples of success stories. If top sales executives are making these things happen, sales managers and reps will see that their leaders are serious about the corporate strategy and will not tolerate mediocrity in its implementation.

Deal Approvers

Deal approvers in an execution-oriented sales organization act as strategic gatekeepers to ensure that exceptional deals are handled in a way that minimizes damage to the bottom line. One way deal approvers can make sure that deals meet "good sale" criteria is to refuse to review any special deal approval requests submitted without a completed Sales Execution Plan. If they don't enforce this rule, the sales team will conclude that although leadership wants the benefits of a sales execution process, the internal compliance system does not support it.

Sales Managers

The sales manager in an execution-oriented sales organization acts like the conductor of a symphony orchestra. She's got the score, she's hired the best musicians available, and she directs them as they learn their parts. Then she drives them to play their best to bring the composer's work alive.

Sales managers have the score—the Sales Execution Plan—and hold their people accountable for following it in order to perform at their highest levels and bring the company's sales strategy to life. Their job is to implement the process at ground level and model the right behavior through disciplined action, ensuring that they have regular sales execution dialogue with the sales team and that the team complies with the requirements.

Sales managers must coach salespeople to make Pivotal Agreements by applying the Dialogue Principles embedded in the Sales Execution Plan. They know that if they model high-performing strategic behavior at every opportunity, profitable deals will emerge. Without their managers modeling and reinforcing the sometimes counterintuitive "right way" on a regular basis, sales representatives fall back into intuitive and unprofitable selling habits.

Sales Professionals

Salespeople work "where the rubber meets the road," at the customer interface. This is where the majority of deal making is initiated, negotiated, and closed. Great sales happen not through persuasion or manipulation, but through knowledge of how the company's products and services solve strategic business issues and add customer value, based on a deep understanding of the customer's business needs.

Sales professionals in execution-oriented selling organizations focus their efforts on using Sales Execution Plans to help them make Pivotal Agreements. They proactively assess what it will take to maximize value at each step in the sales process, and execute each Pivotal Agreement in a way that maximizes results for the organization. If they aren't doing this, they will end up crafting weak agreements with customers early in their sales process that lead to suboptimal revenue growth, poor account profitability, and declining customer satisfaction.

Sales/Customer Support Team

In the execution-oriented sales organization the sales/customer support team has a crucial role in supporting revenue and optimizing margin in every deal. Sometimes this means providing data to the sales team that can be used to enrich the customer dialogue. Sometimes it involves partnering with the sales team to close, implement, or service accounts. The sales/customer support team must provide data and service to support creating profitable deals and encourage customer compliance after the fact. If they don't, well-crafted Sales Execution Plans fail after the deal is made—because members of the support team give things away rather than exchange value during postsale implementation and service.

STRATEGY EXECUTION CHECKLISTS

You can assess and monitor the performance of your sales organization with the extensive checklists I have developed using the framework of the 3D Model: data, dialogue, and discipline. These checklists are provided in the following pages.

Strategy Execution Checklist
TOP SALES EXECUTIVE

Key tasks to embed the 3D Model in the organization

DATA:

- ☐ Take action to ensure that the organization provides data to the sales team that they can use with specific customers to create value-oriented, profit-enhancing dialogue.

- ☐ Require the sales organization to use research in every sale to clarify how their solutions can be positioned to articulate the strategic value that they bring the customer.

- ☐ Identify and report on the metrics associated with sales performance, and embed a strategy execution process that affects ultimate results.

- ☐ Track each element of strategy execution and assign it a target, and then use that data to provide feedback to deal approvers, sales managers, sales representatives, and sales/customer support staff so they can take action to improve results.

- ☐ Put a system in place that uncovers, codifies, and disseminates best practices that foster profitable sales execution.

DIALOGUE:

- ☐ Create an environment in which open, constructive dialogue between sales professionals and their managers is not only encouraged, but required.

- ☐ Intervene when the dialogue isn't happening and re-instill the discipline of focused dialogue.

- ☐ Use the Dialogue Principles in all customer interactions and the planning meetings that precede them; hold everyone in the sales organization responsible for doing the same.

DISCIPLINE:

- ☐ Create a strategy execution plan that focuses on making Pivotal Agreements profitably.

- ☐ Keep score and enforce consequences.

- ☐ Require that all deals reflect the best practices of exemplary performers who have proven their mettle by executing expanded, profitable deals.

- ☐ Insist on the completion of a Sales Execution Plan on any deal you are asked to help with.

- ☐ Implement a process for exceptional deal approval that reinforces the company's focus on profitable corporate strategy execution.

Strategy Execution Checklist
SALES MANAGERS

Key tasks to embed the 3D Model in the organization

DATA:

- ☐ Ensure Pivotal Agreements connect to corporate strategy metrics.

- ☐ Capture, track, and analyze each sales professional's performance on Pivotal Agreement metrics.

- ☐ Collect and share best practices knowledge and make it available to deal makers.

- ☐ Set quantifiable objectives for revenue and margin optimization.

DIALOGUE:

- ☐ Keep the focus on using the Sales Execution Plan to make Pivotal Agreements.

- ☐ Enforce planning processes, and focus sales professionals on creating value by managing information intentionally, identifying and satisfying underlying needs, positioning your solutions advantageously, executing agreements through assessing and exerting power, setting high targets, and exchanging value.

- ☐ Focus on helping sales professionals improve the quality of dialogues with customers at all opportunities—in precall preparation, on sales calls, while coaching in meetings, etc.

DISCIPLINE:

- ☐ Stick to the standards of discipline, including making sales professionals accountable for completing Sales Execution Plans focused on Dialogue Principles and sticking with the plan from the first customer contact to the close of the deal.

- ☐ Build accountability by coaching in a way that gets sales professionals to develop their own execution plans rather than allowing them to "upwardly delegate" problems to management.

- ☐ Help sales professionals identify Pivotal Agreements that must be made at each step in the customer engagement process to advance the sale toward a profitable close.

Strategy Execution Checklist
SALES PROFESSIONALS

Key tasks to embed the 3D Model in the organization

DATA:

- [ ] Use metrics on the customer's buying behavior and contract compliance record, and manage making agreements with these facts in mind.
- [ ] Use best practices data to optimize sales performance.

DIALOGUE:

- [ ] Have a dialogue within the sales organization to identify the Pivotal Agreements that need to be made to move the deal toward a successful close.
- [ ] Use dialoguing opportunities within the sales organization to build a Sales Execution Plan based on the Dialogue Principles that creates value and supports execution of agreements:
  —Manage information intentionally. Anticipate customer action/reaction and plan an appropriate response.
  —Identify and satisfy the underlying needs of the customer and the sales organization.
  —Position your solution advantageously.
  —Focus on making the best possible agreements.
  —Assess and exert your power.
  —Set high targets. Decide on opening, target, and walk-away positions.
  —Exchange value through concessions and trades.
- [ ] Have conversations with customers about positioning your solution in a manner that addresses the customers' strategic needs, while exchanging value, making agreements and trades, and using elegant negotiables.

DISCIPLINE:

- [ ] Assume responsibility for developing Sales Execution Plans rather than asking managers to do so.
- [ ] Complete and review the Sales Execution Plan on a regular basis.
- [ ] Know when to walk away.

Strategy Execution Checklist
DEAL APPROVERS

Key tasks to embed the 3D Model in the organization

DATA:

- ☐ Evaluate the Sales Execution Plan and the results of the deal against known criteria that were set as a guideline to achieve a good price and minimize margin erosion.

- ☐ Provide data to the organization about the number and quality of deals "escalated" for unusual treatment.

- ☐ Approve only those deals that meet the selling criteria of the approved objectives driven by the metrics tied to Pivotal Agreements.

DIALOGUE:

- ☐ Focus conversations about the deal with sales executives, sales managers, and sales professionals on the fundamentals identified in the completed Sales Execution Plan agreements, trades, and concessions.

DISCIPLINE:

- ☐ Understand the corporate strategy and the Dialogue Principles and use that knowledge to evaluate each deal that crosses the desk.

- ☐ Be familiar with the parameters that management has set for what makes an acceptable deal.

- ☐ Evaluate the deal—whether it's inside or outside the parameters— and work with the sales team to reach favorable results.

- ☐ Approve only those deals that result from following a disciplined strategy execution process that uses the Sales Execution Plan and the Dialogue Principles and are in compliance with standards. Send back out-of-compliance deals with confidence, knowing that sales executives will back up the decision.

- ☐ Ask for a completed Sales Execution Plan from the sales representative or sales manager before evaluating any exceptional deal.

Strategy Execution Checklist
SALES/CUSTOMER SUPPORT STAFF

Key tasks to embed the 3D Model in the organization

DATA:

- ☐ Gather, analyze, and report data to the sales organization. Tailor the data to deepen everyone's knowledge of the customer's business needs.

- ☐ Zero in on critical results and process metrics: discounts, customer compliance, and all other factors related to hitting target revenue and increasing margins.

- ☐ Import data into templates where analysts and decision makers can draw conclusions and develop plans for further improving sales execution effectiveness.

DIALOGUE:

- ☐ Probe analysts and decision makers for key data and metrics to track and measure results against.

- ☐ Provide data about the customer to the sales representative that creates the grist for fruitful conversations with the customer.

- ☐ Create and make available an inventory of best practices for making Pivotal Agreements, trades, negotiables, and elegant negotiables.

- ☐ Discuss contract compliance with the facts in hand.

DISCIPLINE:

- ☐ Support the 3D Model and Pivotal Agreements.

Making It Work in the Real World

How can you apply your knowledge of roles and the checklists to the practical world of your sales organization? Here's an example of how one company did it.

This major building materials company needed to increase its gross margins by 5 percent after years of profit erosion. Led by the CEO, each person in the sales organization played a role in achieving the corporate goal. Not only did they achieve their goal to increase gross margins by 5 percent—they exceeded it. Following is the story of how they did it.

- The senior executive articulated the goal and the strategy for getting there and then followed up at regular intervals to ensure that key metrics were moving in the right direction (including data on performance, process compliance, and best practices). In addition, he consistently reviewed completed Sales Execution Plans for key sales opportunities.

- The top sales executive ensured that the sales team had the data, skills, systems, and discipline to get the job done (complete with Sales Execution Plans focused on making Pivotal Agreements).

- Deal approvers (called business development/pricing managers) reviewed exceptional pricing requests from the point of view of profitability and worked with the sales team to implement Sales Execution Plans to maximize margins. A fundamental element of their decisions on whether to approve a deal was whether completed Sales Execution Plans were included with the special offer requests.

- First-line sales managers were directed to have regular, structured "margin conversations" with their salespeople at the point in the sales process when Pivotal Agreements needed to be made. In these structured deal management sessions, the responsibility for creating and implementing Sales Execution Plans using the Dialogue Principles rested with the salesperson.

- Sales professionals were expected to develop Sales Execution Plans that supported every Pivotal Agreement that affected deal profitability and use data provided by the sales support team to structure customer dialogue and maximize margins. Sales Execution Plans were required for all deals worth more than a hundred thousand dollars. The data on margin erosion was available by customer, product, and sales rep to help pinpoint margin improvement opportunities. Sales reps were also expected to have regular margin conversations with their managers, in which they presented plans for how they would maximize returns. What was against the rules? Approaching the manager with a margin-eroding problem without a recommendation for dealing with it—and a plan to execute the recommendation.

- Sales support (in this case a sales operations group) delivered real-time data to the sales team's desktops on account profitability, margin erosion, and other metrics that the team could use in margin-expanding customer dialogue. (Based on this data, for example, a sales rep might be able to deflect a customer's request for an exceptionally low price by pointing out that the customer was already one of the lowest-margin accounts in her region.)

As you can see, the message starts at the top, and cascades through the organization. To consistently achieve great sales that advance the corporate strategy, people at every level in the sales organization must be clear about their own roles and the roles everyone else must play. Then they must exhibit the discipline, employ the data, and engage in the dialogue that will enable them to achieve the goals embedded in the corporate strategy.

Everyone has a role to play. If just one person stumbles—regardless of where in the chain of command—the ultimate relationship will be compromised. I can't emphasize this enough—executing corporate strategy is a team activity.

EARLY WARNING INDICATORS

How do you know if your selling organization isn't using the full potential of its data, dialogue, and discipline to reach its objectives? You'll need to develop your own company-specific list, but here are a few early warning indicators to watch for as you evaluate the results of sales activity:

- Account margins begin to creep in the wrong direction.
- The number of "exception" deals as a percentage of the total increases.

- The average number of back-and-forth "repricing iterations" (between sales, management, and deal approvers) on your deals increases.
- As you walk the halls and participate in sales meetings you discover that people aren't using the terminology of the Dialogue Principles when they talk about their deals.
- During your regular review of the data—which you have linked to the Pivotal Agreements you know need to be made to move deals ahead to a profitable close—you identify patterns and pockets of noncompliance.
- Sales executives are called in to "save the day" on key deals more frequently.
- When executives do get involved in helping close important sales, the focus is on pricing rather than on executing a thorough Sales Execution Plan. There's no mention of the plan, positioning, agreements, or trades.
- Managers are more and more tolerant of mediocrity in deal execution, and seem willing to make costly concessions to customers without a plan for exchanging value.
- You learn that sales professionals are rarely completing Sales Execution Plans.

Now that we've covered the roles of everyone in the organization, in the next chapter, I will explore in detail the role that the C-band leadership plays in moving the sales organization in the right direction.

Summary

The Unbreakable Chain: Linking It Together

- If executing corporate strategy at the point of customer interaction was easy, everyone would do it and there would be no gaps between having a strategy and successfully executing it.

- Everyone has a role in executing corporate strategy. If one individual falters, the sales result will be compromised. Each player must understand his or her role and the consequences of not playing it.

- Without effective leadership, many members of the sales organization will find escape hatches that prevent them from playing their roles in the process. When this happens, the whole process suffers.

- The sales team must understand their individual roles through the lenses of data, dialogue, and discipline. They must adhere to Sales Execution Plans and the Dialogue Principles to help them craft the Pivotal Agreements that lead to the best deals.

- Senior sales executives should develop and monitor early warning indicators that will help them track and manage the execution of the strategy.

8

ALIGNING THE ENTERPRISE

Strive for alignment, not control.

Leading an enterprise to execute its corporate strategy is a very big challenge. When we think of the leader of an enterprise, we might envision the captain of a ship standing on the bridge, giving orders to a highly trained crew. Each crew member—whether he or she is in the engine room, the navigation room, or the officers' dining room—understands his or her place in the hierarchy, and knows his or her role in executing the tasks that result in the ship reaching its destination safely and on time.

But a tightly run ship isn't the reality of most sales organizations. Here's how it frequently plays out in the business world: The CEO and sales leadership meet a number of times in the executive suite or off-site and devise the corporate strategy, often with strategic consulting assistance. They issue directives, give speeches, hold rallies, and everybody hears about the new direction, the new initiative, and the new goals.

Sales professionals—managers, salespeople, deal approvers, sales and customer support staff—interpret this information and take myriad steps to integrate what they think they need to do to incorporate this goal into their daily routines. Things change for a week or two, maybe even a month or a quarter. But before long a new initiative comes down the pike and the sales team shifts their focus, retools, and changes direction yet again.

A few quarters down the line management makes an assessment. The enterprise is not moving in the right direction. Clearly, they are not making the right moves. And so leadership reevaluates, reprioritizes, adds a new system, buys a new training package, hires and fires key personnel—and often reorganizes. Another six months elapse and there is another status check: "Have we made our numbers?" Not quite.

So why doesn't the leader of a business enterprise get the results that the captain of the ship gets? Why doesn't the business enterprise reach its destination—optimal execution of its corporate strategy?

One organization is not equivalent to one ship. Practically speaking, an organization more closely resembles an armada or flotilla. Leading an armada is very different from commanding a single ship. Yet in business today, most sales organizations use the processes, techniques, and tools that were intended to command a single vessel to fix the problems shared by an entire fleet.

Managing a business enterprise is exponentially harder and requires solutions that address the complexity of the problems. Each division, region, and unit fulfills a specific business function with its own character, its own leadership, its own strategy (which may or may not be aligned with the corporate strategy), its own staff, and its own experience base from which it operates and makes decisions.

So in business, it's not just about pointing the ship in the right direction. It's about getting the fleet aligned (fig. 8-1) so that each entity is positioned to do its part in executing the maneuver and achieving the desired outcome. In my experience, the only way to achieve alignment in

FIGURE 8-1   *The key to leading the enterprise is aligning all the entities involved in a strategy execution.*

Making the Shift to an Aligned Sales Organization

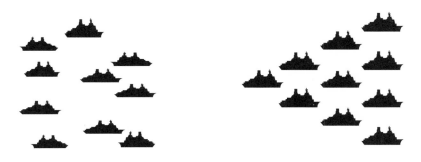

the corporate business environment is to understand where you are, identify where you want to go, and then put the right disciplines and processes in place to make it happen. This is a highly individualized endeavor.

CREATING ALIGNMENT

You can bring your sales organization into alignment through six fundamental activities:

1. Build a mentality of "execution excellence" into your organization.
2. Create an execution blueprint.
3. Deploy the 3D Model.
4. Require discipline in the use of the tools and processes from *The Last Link*.
5. Communicate consistently and regularly with all parts of the organization.
6. Follow up—inspect what you expect.

At each step, there will be opportunities to use the concepts and tools I've introduced in this book: Pivotal Agreements, the 3D Model, Sales Execution Plans, and the Dialogue Principles.

Let's look at each of these activities in a little more detail.

Build a Mentality of "Execution Excellence" into Your Organization

First and foremost, you need to get the organization mentally ready to receive new strategy execution tools, processes, and measurements. In order to get your organization ready, you and your executive team need to be mentally ready. You need to adopt an execution excellence mentality yourself.

To do that, you must assess the gap between your strategy and what is required to successfully execute your strategy. Furthermore, you need to evaluate the potential return on investment from successfully executing corporate strategy and create a high-level approach to project sponsorship (by getting your entire executive team on board) with appropriate organization-wide communication and deployment. How can you do these things?

- Own and manage sales execution.
- Deploy organization-wide discipline focused on making Pivotal Agreements.
- Refuse to tolerate mediocrity or noncompliance.
- Build accountability through good leadership and change management.

Create an Execution Blueprint

Once you have mentally prepared your organization and your executive team is on board with the new strategy execution processes and the requirements to make them work, you need to create and implement a blueprint that reflects everything that needs to get done (and who needs to do it) to successfully embed and deploy the methodology. This will involve studying the corporate strategy, understanding the implications of executing the strategy within the sales organization, and assessing current business practices, opportunities, and roadblocks. When you know and understand the current state of all these elements, you and your executive team must rewire your sales organization to use and embrace the strategy execution processes and tools.

Your blueprint needs to do the following:

- Connect all of your sales execution activities directly to your strategic sales initiative(s).
- Leverage existing "need/pain" data to identify problems and solution sets.
- Identify the Pivotal Agreements upon which the size and profitability of the sale rests for each business group in the company.
- Integrate the deal management tools (Sales Execution Plans, the Dialogue Principles, and the 3D Model) into your current sales management processes and systems.
- Describe how you will hold your people accountable for complying with the initiative.
- Propose ways to garner executive sponsorship and communicate the strategy to all those responsible for achieving it.
- Specify methods for tracking and reporting results.
- Direct the planning and management activities required to facilitate achieving the strategic initiative at the point of customer contact.

You may need to bring in professional help to create this kind of blueprint. An execution specialist can help you objectively assess systems and processes, and, most important, identify the right Pivotal Agreements you will need to make to successfully achieve your strategic goals at the point of customer contact.

Deploy the Processes and Tools Outlined in *The Last Link*

When you have a detailed blueprint to follow, you are ready to deploy the 3D Model, Dialogue Principles, and Sales Execution Plans. Your execution process should focus your people on planning and executing Pivotal Agreements. Measure, monitor, and modify it as implementation progresses.

A small percentage of the agreements you make—the Pivotal Agreements—will likely yield 80 percent of the financial rewards. So you need to embed the discipline that focuses on making those Pivotal Agreements into

---

Elements of Discipline

1. Uses structured Sales Execution Plans
2. Focuses on making the Pivotal Agreements connected to financial metrics by using data and dialogue to carry out corporate strategy
3. Uses the Dialogue Principles and related best practices
4. Is deployed through existing sales management processes and systems
5. Is sponsored by the top sales executive and sales leadership team
6. Is reinforced and measured by management

---

the daily sales planning practices of your sales force. If your sales force is not working on identifying and making Pivotal Agreements, they aren't working on the right things to make your organization profitable.

You cannot make good agreements unless you are applying the Dialogue Principles. Create structures, policies, processes, procedures, and reward systems in your organization to ensure that sales and sales support personnel use Sales Execution Plans when planning and executing agreements.

Require the Use of the Strategy Execution Tools

For deal makers—and I mean anyone who participates in making deals, not just the sales professionals who face customers—the specific strategy execution tools that need to be implemented at this point include access to best practices and a Sales Execution Plan that addresses the metrics linked to Pivotal Agreements.

For managers—sales managers, sales leadership, and the C-level support group—the necessary tools include guidelines for leading meetings and ensuring that discussion focuses on the deal management dialogue. Because managers are often called to consult on or participate in key customer calls, they must also have a deep understanding of the Dialogue Principles and have access to the same tools that deal makers have and use.

Communicate Consistently and Regularly with All Parts of Your Organization

Regular and consistent communication is an essential part of leading your enterprise to successfully execute your corporate strategy.

Align the messages about the corporate strategy and the sales execution strategy you send to all parts of your organization. Management messages that swing back and forth between profit, volume, product launch, and market share are confusing. Division leaders frequently react and create goals that are at cross-purposes. For example, when sales focuses on volume and contracting focuses on margins and marketing is worried about market share, these groups will be working at cross-purposes, frantically trying to make their numbers. A win in sales will result in a loss in contracting. Take the time to think through the messages you are sending and make sure they are consistent so that each segment of the organization is working toward the same goal.

Be clear about what needs changing. State what needs to change in terms of metrics. For example, "We need to improve margins by reducing discounts by 18 percent." Explain why you need to change, for example, "A 1 percent improvement in price creates an improvement in operating profit of 11.1 percent." Be specific about content; tailor communications precisely for your target audiences.

Follow Up—Inspect What You Expect

When you've implemented all these changes to your organization, you must follow up. As a functional "owner" responsible for sales execution you must "inspect what you expect." The most powerful enabler for your new sales initiative is management attention. You cannot expect compliance with the sales execution standards if you are not paying attention. You cannot set a new standard and then revert to business as usual. Vote with your time by inspecting for what you expect.

One CEO we worked with launched an initiative to improve cash flow. He made it a daily practice to question sales professionals and sales support staff about the payment terms they negotiated with customers, and then examined whether or not customers were in compliance. Every weekly, monthly, and quarterly sales meeting had cash flow and payment compliance on the agenda. Eventually the importance of cash flow became so ingrained in the daily thinking of this sales organization that they became expert at negotiating payment terms and collecting what was due.

It is critical to regularly reinforce the need to use the strategy execution tools to make Pivotal Agreements; leverage data, dialogue, and discipline; use Sales Execution Plans and the Dialogue Principles; and set performance-oriented strategy execution goals. So is insisting upon regular deal management coaching conversations between sales managers and sales reps.

Reinforce the use of the strategy execution tools and methods on an ongoing basis to ensure that your people do not fall back into bad habits during moments of crisis or adversity. Use coaching techniques and senior management interventions to remind your organization that you are serious about the new business order.

COUNTERINTUITIVE CHANGE MANAGEMENT

Doing the right things to create the change you want can often be counterintuitive.

It is counterintuitive to take the time and make the effort to inspect what you expect. It's intuitive to lay down the law and then delegate its enforcement. Just like good parenting, good management involves direct and frequent involvement.

It is counterintuitive to ensure that people comply with the process instead of simply focusing on results. It's intuitive for managers to talk about making their numbers. They don't talk about how they got there and how they might improve their process, they just focus on the close—the results. It's counterintuitive to break down the sales process into executable agreements and then manage a process to create better agreements.

It is counterintuitive to work for alignment rather than control. It is intuitive to strive for control and actually believe you can achieve it, but creating alignment focused on strategy execution for your organization is the only way to really make it happen.

It is counterintuitive to focus on optimizing the Pivotal Agreements rather than try to master all aspects of deal making or win every point that's up for negotiation. And yet time after time we've seen that when an organization executes the Pivotal Agreements correctly, the outcome of the sale is far superior.

It is counterintuitive to add another process to supplement your organization's existing sales processes. I can hear the groans in the sales meeting now. "Another process? More time? More make-work? More hoops to jump through? I think I'll pass." But in fact, if the 3D Model focuses your sales organization on planning the sale and executing the Pivotal Agreements throughout the sales process, you are actually going to reduce sales cycle time significantly and create a better sales outcome.

How, you ask? First, consider the consistent revenue and margin erosion that your sales force is unwittingly adding to on a daily basis. Think about the countless discounts and giveaways (which typically show up in price waterfall audits) that are lost because there is not a required strategy execution process in place to focus the salesperson on doing the right things to avoid these critical revenue and margin leakages.

Think about your nonstandard deal approval process and how many iterations occur back and forth between sales and deal approvers before a deal can be accepted or rejected. In my experience the sales cycle time can be cut by 40 percent or more by getting the plan right the first time. Think about how much sales cycle time could be reduced if your sales force was required to submit a complete, comprehensive Sales Execution Plan when the initial deal approval request was made. Not just any strategy execution process, but the 3D Model that enables your salespeople to reduce their sales cycle time and maximize revenue and margin opportunity.

Is it counterintuitive to add steps to the sales process? You bet. But it works. And the end result is that you will have positioned your salespeople to be faster and more agile, responding to the changing demands of the marketplace. The architects of any strategy execution initiative have to think in a counterintuitive way to get the right results.

GET THE HELP YOU NEED

When appropriate, it certainly makes sense to bring in strategy execution experts from the outside to help you assess your situation and point you in the right direction. Outside experts can often give you the perspective you need to sort through all facets of the problem and get the organization on track to implement the right solution. In all likelihood you will need to engage an outside specialist if you have specifically targeted revenue and margin optimization in your corporate strategy.

But first a word of caution. These outside experts are not necessarily the same consulting resources that typically help organizations identify problems and make recommendations for change. You will need experts who understand at a tactical level how to close the gap between having a strategy and effectively executing it. These experts must know how to break the sales process down into a series of key agreements that, when executed properly, create the best outcomes. They need to be able to quantify the projected margin contribution. They need to understand and be able to help you deploy and embed the right kind of discipline, as well as provide ongoing strategy execution reinforcement that will change the behavior of your sales force. They need to be able to support your efforts to instill continuous communication and coaching to ensure that you meet your financial improvement goals. Lastly, they need to be able to help you deploy revenue and margin optimization measurement processes to take the metrics that you want improved and connect them to the overall corporate strategy execution approach.

When selecting an execution specialist, ask about the process they engage in to uncover Pivotal Agreements; have them explain the principles and behaviors they plan to elicit and find out how they do this; question them about processes they embed to ensure ongoing results; and finally, request specific data on how and to what degree they have helped sales teams maximize return on investment.

FIVE ALIGNMENT OPPORTUNITIES
THAT PRODUCE IMMEDIATE RESULTS

There are five things I recommend you work on immediately to align your sales team's activities with your corporate strategy. When you can take advantage of the alignment opportunities below, you'll start to see a dramatic shift in behavior and outcomes.

The Plan Align the team involved in making and managing the sale with the plan and its execution to ensure that the customer is always presented with a united front. Don't give your customer an opportunity to divide and conquer. Aligning with the plan, especially where Pivotal Agreements are concerned, also reduces the time and energy spent haggling internally about pricing, trades, and concessions.

Language/Approach Align sales professionals by introducing and using a common approach and common language to manage the sales process up and down your organization. Your people should be talking about positioning, targets, Pivotal Agreements, trades, concessions, and negotiables all the time.

Multiple Product/Service Solutions Align the different groups in your organization who provide the components of a multiple product/service solution (e.g., software plus financing) so that they are working in tandem, not at cross-purposes. Remember, the higher business purpose is providing the greatest solution value for the customer. Make sure all your product/service solution teams understand this and support each other's success, both as individuals and as parts of the organization. And if you ask for this type of performance behavior, reward it.

Incentives Align your incentive program with the successful execution of your company strategy at the point of customer interface. If you are working on improving margins, do not reward your people on gross revenue results. Reward them on net results. Think about rewards and incentives before you put them in place, and remember that money, though important, is not the sole motivator. For many, intangibles—respect, courtesy, professionalism, the pride that comes with adding value, and the recognition that results from doing things right and creating success—provide a huge incentive to adopt new strategies and excel at applying them.

Control Systems Align your measurement criteria and your tracking and reporting processes with the strategy and results you are trying to achieve. Put the proper control systems in place so that you can monitor and report results, and then take appropriate action to revise and fine-tune your sales execution strategy.

WHAT IT LOOKS LIKE WHEN YOU'RE DOING IT RIGHT

Just as there are early warning indicators that things are going wrong, there are early indicators that success is at hand.

When a global technology company started using Sales Execution Plans including the Dialogue Principles, it realized immediate results: Its initiative was designed to lower discounts and halt the steady margin erosion it had been experiencing for nine straight quarters. After learning and applying all of the strategy execution tools described in *The Last Link*, this organization reduced solution discounting by 14 percent in two short quarters. Each discount point meant $12 million in annual profit. Over three quarters, the net increase in profit was just short of $40 million.

This is not an uncommon story. Early successes create momentum. Success begets success, and early success accelerates the ultimate success of the initiative. The buzz starts, there is excitement and buy-in, and everyone wants to be affiliated with it. Soon a larger and larger percentage of the total sales organization is using the methodologies of *The Last Link*. And before you know it—the numbers start moving in the right direction.

Those who are disciplined, use their data, and have focused dialogue will reap their rewards.

The Last Link Discipline Tool Kit:
What You Need to Close the Gap

- Pivotal Agreements
- The 3D Model: data, dialogue, discipline
- Dialogue Principles
- Sales Execution Plans

Summary

The Unbreakable Chain: Aligning the Enterprise

- You must incorporate an "excellence in execution" mentality into your sales organization. Introduce a tailored approach to your company's sales strategy planning process and the appropriate management tools that help people perform at their greatest potential. Constantly reinforce the use of those tools by monitoring performance — inspect for what you expect.

- The right thing to do in a sales organization is often the counterintuitive thing to do. Assess the gap between the strategy you currently have and the strategic results you want. Then apply the 3D Model to help make the changes you want and empower your sales organization to stop, listen, and think — using data, dialogue, discipline, Sales Execution Plans, and the Dialogue Principles to optimize Pivotal Agreements — before they act.

- Explain the desired outcome to all players. Be specific. You won't get what you don't ask for.

9

ADOPTING THE TOOLS OF
THE LAST LINK

*Your success depends on the degree to which everyone, at all levels in the
organization, understands and consistently complies with the game plan.*

BUSINESS AS USUAL

Successfully and consistently executing corporate strategy at the point of
customer interface is an ongoing process. It requires diligence, intent, and
consistent care and maintenance.

Most organizations begin full of excitement, hope, and promise. They
discover a disconnect between what they should be doing and what they
are doing, and they make a monumental effort up front. They study the
problem, they craft the strategy they believe will yield improved revenue
and margins, and then they announce the strategy.

Unfortunately, once organizations release the strategy, all too often they
let the effort end there. Instead of fully linking the strategy to their everyday

business practices, they falter. The urgency that caused everyone to focus on defining the problem is diffused. Resources are scattered, expertise is applied to other issues, and budgets are spent to solve *new* corporate challenges. The gap between what could be and what is widens.

At a critical juncture—when leadership should be connecting the people, resources, processes, and standards that will enable them to effectively execute their strategy—they lose focus and will. This break ultimately sabotages the entire process.

THE NEED TO CONNECT

It's not enough to have a strategy. Research shows that only 10 percent of formulated strategies are executed successfully. You've got to carry it out—connect it to the day-to-day activities that make the difference in your bottom line. The most important thing you can do to successfully execute your corporate strategy is to identify and make Pivotal Agreements at the point of customer interaction.

To make those Pivotal Agreements, start with data. Gather and use it effectively. Generate the key financial metrics that your strategy is designed to affect. If you're trying to stop a price waterfall, quantify which data points reflect the leakage. Isolate and track that data as you book future sales. This is the information that will tell you whether or not your execution methods are creating the desired result.

Examples of data that will help your sales team include customer buy records, payment records, contract compliance records, financing records, and demurrage records. Your sales team should have at their fingertips all the data they need to be able to clearly and compellingly state how their product or service matches the customer's business needs. With this data your sales team can plan, position, and sell your value to optimize revenue and margins with each customer.

Ultimately, your data needs to support the critical dialogues between the deal makers and the customers. These conversations are where the strategy and successful sales execution connect, where the agreements that determine the size and profitability of the sale are made.

Apply the Dialogue Principles to deal conversations when you make these agreements. Position your solution's value while meeting customer needs (not customer wants); focus on the Pivotal Agreements that lead to results; set high targets; manage information flow; assess and exert your power; decide on your concession strategies as part of the Sales Execution Plan; identify and make trades using primary, alternative, and elegant negotiables. When your entire sales organization understands and uses Dialogue Principles to make Pivotal Agreements, they will be fully prepared for this critical customer dialogue, regardless of when, where, and with whom it takes place.

Finally, be disciplined and run a disciplined organization. Have the discipline to own and manage execution of the corporate strategy. Hold people accountable for applying the appropriate strategy execution methodology. Use the tools yourself and require every other sales professional in your organization to use them. Structure and plan the approach you will take to sell each customer the business solution that only you can provide. And when you've implemented the entire process, have the discipline to inspect what you expect.

IT'S ABOUT MORE THAN JUST SELLING

There is more at stake here than making a sale or losing a sale.

When you hold your people accountable and give them the right tools and support to do their jobs, they become responsible, empowered, fully functioning sales professionals capable of optimally executing corporate strategy and achieving amazing results.

Furthermore, when you send an empowered sales force out, they will be able to turn a sales opportunity into a strategic partnership by providing thoughtful solutions to help customers solve their business problems. The give-and-take of assessing needs and making agreements, trades, and concessions leads to mutual respect between sellers and buyers. Mutual respect deepens relationships. When you partner this way with customers, you increase their commitment and desire to do business with you. And there is virtually no way your competitors will be able to drive a wedge between you and your customer—regardless of their tactics.

If you partner this way with your customers, the benefits may even reach beyond either of your businesses to the community at large. Consider this story about one of our clients, a major communications company. Their client's mandate was that all major governmental entities must have excellent communication systems at all times—particularly in times of emergency. A person's life often depends on the capacity of the communications system to effectively transmit critical information from multiple places to multiple parties within seconds.

We all know cities are tight with their budget dollars—for good reason. So it's not unusual for communications companies to receive requests to bid on projects, setting up a bidding war based on price.

Before they adopted our approach to executing sales, this company would have responded to the pricing request. But armed with the conviction that comes from understanding and using the Dialogue Principles, they made a Pivotal Agreement to gain access to the critical decision-makers and demonstrate that they thoroughly understood the city's problems and needs before they submitted their bid.

The result was that they were able to help their customer develop a coherent communications strategy. And instead of selling the city a few devices at a time, substantially increasing the total cost of ownership as well as increasing major risk relative to a critical need—reliable communications 24/7—our client was able to sell the city a total communications solution. It was a sale worth more than $10 million.

THE LAST WORD

M. Scott Peck began his epic best-selling book *The Road Less Traveled* with these words: "Life is difficult."[1] I don't know about you, but when I read those words, I felt a great sense of relief. Finally, here was someone telling it like it is. Someone who wasn't trying to sugar-coat reality by getting people to believe that at some point living the good life was easy—or should be.

Yes, life is challenging. Work is challenging. Leading an organization is challenging. And executing corporate strategy is challenging. But as Peck counsels, when we acknowledge the challenge and the pain, we can prepare ourselves for the challenge in the best way possible.

This book presents a simple, powerful approach to achieving your corporate strategy that will prepare you and your team for the challenges you face. Every strategy execution initiative is unique to its organization. However, using the methodologies in *The Last Link*—Sales Execution Plans, the Dialogue Principles, and the 3D Model for making Pivotal Agreements—to achieve your corporate strategy will close the gap in your sales process and yield the bottom-line results you are looking for.

But be forewarned: there are no shortcuts. You must be willing to commit to leading the way and ensuring that the work gets done, reinforcing the approach consistently, holding people accountable to do their parts, and sticking with the methods even when it's difficult. Your success depends on the degree to which everyone, at all levels in the organization, understands and consistently complies with the game plan.

Connecting your sales process to strategy is not without its challenges. There is no silver bullet. You've got to do the work. The unbreakable sales organization you'll achieve in the end, however, is well worth the effort. If you embrace this new strategy execution model today and start using the tools in *The Last Link*, your numbers are going to start moving in the right direction—and future calls with the Wall Street analysts will be much more positive.

Good luck!

APPLICATION: *THE LAST LINK* WORKBOOK

This application section provides supplemental strategy execution information and gives you an opportunity to apply key concepts from the book to test your comprehension and readiness.

- **Course A: The Importance of Business Acumen** reviews essential business knowledge that high-performing executives, sales managers, and sales professionals must possess in order to carry out corporate strategy at the customer interface. (This section should be required reading for sales managers and sales professionals.)

- **Course B: The Change Factor** provides a brief but comprehensive review of change management principles. As you work to close the gap between strategy and its execution, you may decide to facilitate changes in your organization. In this course, I describe basic approaches and offer advice to help you initiate a change management initiative.

- **Course C: Reality Selling** presents a realistic but fictional case study involving a Fortune 200 company (Digital Widgets, Inc.) that is facing the challenges of executing its corporate strategy at the customer interface. At the end of the case, you will have an opportunity to apply all of the concepts that you've learned throughout this book (including the lessons from the application section). You will be asked to diagnose problems, identify what went wrong at Digital Widgets, Inc., and prescribe solutions. This course can be used as a training tool with all members of a sales organization.

COURSE A

The Importance of Business Acumen

I've observed that truly great performers have excellent business acumen: they know why and how their prospects buy, they do their research and review the data, they understand the financials, and they put their knowledge to work. They use these skills to obtain and analyze information—data—about their customers. Then they use the data in turn to create compelling dialogue using the Dialogue Principles, and to create value, which leads to optimized revenues and margins.

Time and time again, I've seen that the best performers engage in this disciplined process on a regular and consistent basis. As a result, they significantly enhance their ability to successfully execute company strategy when they are face-to-face with the customer.

As most executives know, you develop business acumen—keen insight and mental sharpness—by "going to school" on the fundamentals of how business works in today's competitive environment. This course contains quick-start basics that you can use to develop and sharpen your business acumen. We will focus on how to gain knowledge of your customer's key strategic and financial issues and how to translate this information into results at the customer interface.

Knowledge of a customer's financial and strategic concerns—and the ability to position your products and services within this context—is essential to executing strategy.

WHO WANTS TO BUY FROM YOU?

The primary criterion for a buy decision is this: does it represent a solution? Does it solve a problem? Does it mitigate a strategic challenge we are facing? Vendors need to understand that solutions are the central issue, not their product.
—COO, Fortune 100 company

Behind all the glitz and glamour—the branding that corporations like to project to their public—there are hard-core business fundamentals that every organization needs to address and manage. These fundamentals are divided into "structural" and "execution" components.

The structural fundamentals include strong, reliable products that people want to buy; a cost-effective way to produce and deliver those products; the ability to recognize markets and opportunities; and a corporate strategy to bring the products or solutions to the marketplace.

The execution component encompasses all the processes and actions that must occur in order for companies to successfully deploy their corporate strategy at the customer interface, where returns are increased and maximized. Execution requires a disciplined sales process that is directly connected to the key performance metrics that determine organizational success—earnings, growth, return on investment, and the resulting increase in shareholder value.

Every business must be positioned to successfully address all components of these structural and execution fundamentals if it is to thrive, grow, and compete. It stands to reason, then, that all purchasing decisions ultimately depend on whether or not the customers believe the product or service being sold to them represents a solution to a business need (either structural or execution) and that it will help them

- Improve performance (their own and their customers')
- Increase earnings
- Increase revenue growth
- Increase return on investment
- Increase shareholder value

Prospects want to buy from sellers who can create economic value for them and their customers. What do we mean by "creating economic value"?

- Your solution helps your customer solve a business problem and leads to increased revenue, reduction in expense, improved profitability efficiency, or reduced process complexity.

- Your solution helps your customer help her customers solve a business problem that leads to increased revenue, reduction in expense, improved profitability efficiency, or reduced process complexity.

- Your solution leads to increased revenue and margins for your customer, and ideally your customer's customer.

Sellers who are able to demonstrate economic value to prospects create economic value for their own companies as well, because they sell to the customers' true needs and so have a better opportunity to maximize the customer solution set being sold. We call it the "Economic Value Food Chain." Make sure you are a part of the Economic Value Food Chain by following these simple steps to build your business acumen.

1. Investigate your prospect's business, goals and objectives, strategy, and financials.

2. Analyze the information you've gathered. Develop an in-depth understanding of the prospect's business and their position in the marketplace; know why the company is distinctive, and find out

if they're faltering; learn what they are trying to accomplish and how they plan to do it.

3. Find opportunities to frame and position how your solution will help your prospective customer increase his company's performance (financial results), as well as his customers' performance.

4. Make the deal using the tools provided in this book: Pivotal Agreements; the 3D Model—data, dialogue, and discipline; Sales Execution Plans; and the Dialogue Principles.

Your objective should be to know enough about your prospect that you can position your solution to demonstrate that you not only understand their business, but you are providing a business solution that will help them improve their financial performance and, ideally, their customers' financial performance.

INVESTIGATE AND REVIEW THE DATA

Before you pick up the phone and make that first contact, do your research. Don't walk into a selling situation as a tabula rasa—a blank slate—and think you can win the business based on the strength of your personality or relationships. Besides your positioning theme and your in-depth knowledge of the features and benefits of your product or service, you need to know enough about your prospect's company to make a value-added pitch.

In addition to gathering information about your customer from your marketing department, use the Internet to research your prospective customer, its industry, and its customers. Internet research can also be an invaluable addition to internal resources and data about past contracts, style of contract negotiation, size of purchases, and purchasing cycles if you are looking to expand your relationship with an existing customer. The key to the size and quality of sales is the degree to which you prepare, use collected data, and plan the execution of your sales strategy.

Here are a few suggestions to get you moving in the right direction. Go to your prospect's website. Most companies now have a website that provides a wealth of information about the company's purpose, its strategic direction, the products and services it sells, how its products represent solution sets that meet its customers' needs, and basic information about the industries it is selling into and its management team, as well as myriad links to other resources. In addition, all publicly held companies provide researchers (that's you!) instant access to their company's financials, quarterly earnings, and stock price information as well as their annual reports, an excellent source of information about challenges and risks associated with attaining their strategic goals.

Most large companies have a "press room" that provides links to recent press releases about new products, management changes, new directions, etc. Furthermore, there are often company presentations on the website (typically found in the Investor Relations section of the website) that provide valuable information regarding key strategic initiatives or issues the company faces.

Figures A-1 and A-2 show two different views of Hewlett-Packard's corporate website. The first provides links to company information and the second shows the Investor Relations drop-down menu.

Aside from the company's website, there are literally thousands of resources at your fingertips. Figure A-3 lists a number of domestic and international sources to help you jump-start your search for information.

Gain Insight into Strategic Plans

As you conduct your investigation, you should gain insight into your customer's goals and strategic plan.

Your customers' goals and objectives are driven by external factors— things like the economy, competition, changes in technology, customer needs and expectations, availability of resources, and changing regulations—and by the goals and objectives of their customers.

All of these factors cause prospects to adapt. And their strategy defines the course of action. How do you find out what your prospect organization's current strategy is and how they are doing on their execution? As I mentioned before, the websites of publicly held companies offer great

FIGURE A-1 *Corporate websites provide general information about your prospect.*

FIGURE A-2 *Detailed financial information is often available on the company's website under Investor Relations.*

» Company information

» About us
» Newsroom
» Corporate executive team
» Global citizenship
» HP Labs
» Industry analyst relations
» Investor relations

» About us
  » Accessibility
  » Corporate objectives
  » Diversity & Inclusion
  » Executive Briefing
    Centers
  » Government & Public
    Affairs
  » Headquarters
  » History & Facts
  » Intellectual property
    licensing
  » Investments
  » Jobs at HP
  » Sponsorships
  » Student information

» Company information

**» HP Investor relations
   home**

Company financials
  » Annual report
  » Quarterly results
  » SEC filings
  » Order financials
  » E-delivery

Investor resources
  » Contact us
  » Dividend reinvestment
    plan
  » FAQs
  » Upcoming events
  » Mergers & Acquisitions
  » Risk factors
  » Stock information

Corporate governance
  » Corporate governance
    guidelines
  » Standards of business
    conduct
  » Board of directors
  » Board structure and
    Committees
  » Section 16 filings
  » Bylaws and Certificate
    of incorporation

  » Executive team
  » Newsroom
  » Global citizenship
    report

FIGURE A-3 *Here is a sampling of the myriad resources that can provide you with information to improve your understanding of your prospect's company.*

Information at Your Fingertips	
Domestic sources	• Networked contacts outside or inside of the customer organization • 10K, 10Q—10K Wizard, Edgar Online • Analyst reports—Lehman Research, Merrill Lynch, Morgan Stanley (or any brokerage firm) • Business research links—Hoovers; NYSE; NASDAQ; Nikkei; MSN; CBS Marketwatch; Ameritrade; Yahoo! Finance; newspapers; business magazines and periodicals • Business magazines—*Business Week, Economist, Fast Company, Forbes, Institutional Investor, Wired* • Ratings—A.M. Best, Moody's, Standard & Poor's • Internet search—Google, Yahoo, etc.
International sources	• Global Edge (globaledge.msu.edu) • U.S. Commercial Service, Market Research Library (buyusainfo.net) • CAROL—online annual reports (carol.co.uk) • Corporate Information (www.corporateinformation.com) • Corporate Direct (www.c-direct.ne.jp) • Bloomberg (www.bloomberg.com)

resources in their Investor Relations sections. Often there are transcripts, PowerPoint presentations, or actual recordings of the latest call with Wall Street analysts. These calls occur on a quarterly basis and can provide an enterprising researcher with much information about the company, its plans, its prospects, and what factors are of concern to Wall Street. If you're dealing with a private company, search their website for clues about their business issues, strategies, target markets, and product/service offerings. Try contacting customers and suppliers of your prospects to gain greater insight into their culture, buying behavior, and any challenges or barriers to success they may be experiencing.

Be aware that strategy, goals, and objectives within an organization often differ by division, level, and function. Depending on the product or service you are selling, this may represent an opportunity to get them in alignment.

Look at the Financials

Until you understand a company's financials, you won't have a full picture of the company's health, its challenges and vulnerabilities, and the general direction it is headed. Reviewing a company's financials—income statements, operating statements, and balance sheets—and truly understanding the underlying meaning of the numbers will give you a leg up on your competitors when it comes to positioning value.

Financial Statement Fundamentals

The **balance sheet** (fig. A-4) gives you a snapshot of the company's financial position at a point in time. Key issues include how the business is being financed (What is the capital structure of the company? Is the company highly leveraged or is there little debt on the books?), how much liquidity the company has, and what components of working capital are using the most cash.

Balance Sheet 101

A balance sheet represents the book value of the assets owned by a company and how those assets were financed. Two companies that are identical in every way can choose different ways to finance their assets. Some companies choose to have more debt as part of their capital structure, while others prefer to have lower debt levels. The general risk inherent in the assets owned by the company should determine how much risk a company can prudently have in its balance sheet. Some debt provides greater leverage and can enhance profitable growth, but too much debt can slow growth as liquidity and going concern issues arise.

FIGURE A-4 *The balance sheet*

DIGITAL WIDGETS, INC.
CONSOLIDATED BALANCE SHEETS
(in thousands, except share and per share amounts)

| | December 31 | |
	2004	2003
ASSETS		
Current assets:		
Cash and cash equivalents	$ 7,755	$ 11,703
Accounts receivable, net of allowance for doubtful accounts of $8,688 and $9,758 respectively	81,003	83,553
Inventories, net of allowance for reserves of $4,033 and $3,318 respectively	33,468	33,373
Costs and estimated earnings in excess of billings on uncompleted contracts	11,469	15,218
Deferred tax asset	3,443	4,521
Other current assets	8,008	8,856
Total current assets	$145,146	$157,224
Property, plant and equipment, net	24,391	28,948
Goodwill, net	317,308	308,158
Intangibles, net	24,622	24,591
Other assets	2,108	3,356
Total assets	$513,575	$522,277

(continued on next page)

(continued from previous page)

DIGITAL WIDGETS, INC.
CONSOLIDATED BALANCE SHEETS
(in thousands, except share and per share amounts)

	December 31 2004	2003
LIABILITIES AND STOCKHOLDERS' EQUITY		
Current liabilities:		
Current debt	$ 884	$ 772
Accounts payable	25,591	25,423
Billings in excess of costs and estimated earnings on uncompleted contracts	4,721	2,746
Accrued compensation and benefits	5,697	5,717
Accrued restructuring expenses	494	5,151
Other accrued expenses	13,488	16,137
Accrued income taxes	3,079	2,450
Total current liabilities	$ 53,954	$ 58,396
Long-term debt	29,314	41,211
Deferred taxes	9,208	10,228
Other liabilities	345	423
Stockholders' equity:		
Preferred stock authorized 5,000,000; par value $1.00; none issued and outstanding	—	—
Common stock authorized 100,000,000; par value $.001; issued 19,393,678 and 19,194,034 shares respectively; outstanding 17,859,330 and 18,771,534 shares respectively	19	19
Additional paid-in capital	270,183	246,059
Retained earnings	335,563	299,198
Treasury stock, at cost, 5,534,348 and 3,822,500 shares respectively	(199,904)	(136,289)
Accumulated other comprehensive income	14,893	3,032
Total stockholders' equity	420,754	412,019
Total liabilities and stockholders' equity	$513,575	$522,277

The **income statement** (fig. A-5) tells you what happened during a period of time. It provides a good basis for understanding how the business is performing. Key things to look at on an income statement: Is the business growing? How has profitability been progressing? What is happening to gross margins, expense margins, and profit margins?

FIGURE A-5   *The income statement*

DIGITAL WIDGETS, INC.
CONSOLIDATED STATEMENT OF INCOME
(in thousands, except share and per share amounts)

	Year ended December 31		
	2004	2003	2002
REVENUES	$433,677	$504,181	$619,734
Cost of sales	253,468	305,142	377,609
Gross profit	180,209	199,039	242,125
Selling, general, and administrative expenses	117,338	127,340	151,556
Restructuring expense	—	5,447	2,917
Intangibles amortization	205	314	142
Operating income	62,666	65,938	87,510
Interest expense, net	1,507	2,355	5,223
Other expense, net	123	191	229
Income before income taxes	61,036	63,392	82,058
Provision for income taxes	21,668	22,822	30,357
Net income	$ 39,368	$ 40,570	$ 51,701
Basic earnings per common share	$ 2.17	$ 2.05	$ 2.59
Diluted earnings per common share	$ 2.10	$ 1.99	$ 2.48
Weighted average common shares	18,173	19,781	19,936
Weighted average common and common equivalent shares	18,766	20,342	20,860
Dividends declared per common share	$ 0.17	$ 0.08	$ —

The **statement of cash flows** (fig. A-6) shows how much cash the company generated (or required) and what its sources and uses of cash were. Remember, the income statement provides a long-term measure of the company's success or failure. Cash is king. Without it a company closes its doors. It is important to note the connection between cash flow and the working capital requirements of a business.

FIGURE A-6   *Statement of cash flows*

DIGITAL WIDGETS, INC.
CONSOLIDATED STATEMENT OF CASH FLOWS
(in thousands)

	Year ended December 31		
	2004	2003	2002
CASH FLOWS FROM OPERATING ACTIVITIES			
Net income	$39,368	$ 40,570	$ 51,701
Adjustments to reconcile net income to cash provided by operating activities:			
Depreciation and amortization	5,638	6,680	6,911
Gain on sale of property	(443)	—	—
Deferred tax provision/(benefit)	1,988	(6,509)	—
Tax benefit from exercised options	(5,658)	(1,518)	(2,198)
Changes in working capital items:			
Accounts receivable, net	6,238	19,259	42,978
Inventories, net	953	6,662	4,753
Other current assets	14,557	23,248	4,740
Accounts payable	302	(5,598)	(34,009)
Accrued compensation and benefits	(36)	(2,191)	(6,733)
Accrued expenses	(3,558)	(8,438)	(460)
Accrued income taxes	1,134	(319)	(9,658)
Other long-term liabilities	1,978	5,301	(1,898)
Cash provided by operating activities	62,462	77,148	56,128

(continued on next page)

(continued from previous page)

DIGITAL WIDGETS, INC.
CONSOLIDATED STATEMENT OF CASH FLOWS
(in thousands)

	Year ended December 31		
	2004	2003	2002
CASH FLOWS FROM INVESTING ACTIVITIES			
Capital expenditures	$ (1,394)	$ (1,298)	$ (3,164)
Capital disposals	1,543	1,044	2,338
Merger transactions and prior merger-related payments, net of cash acquired of $0, $1,459 and $7,050 respectively	(2,508)	(6,518)	(16,143)
Cash used in investing activities	(2,359)	(6,772)	(16,970)
CASH FLOWS FROM FINANCING ACTIVITIES			
Repayment of borrowings	(191,595)	(110,388)	(158,675)
Proceeds from borrowings	179,667	86,458	116,250
Proceeds from the exercise of options	18,466	3,973	9,659
Payment of dividends	(3,053)	(813)	—
Purchase of treasury stock	(67,548)	(48,728)	—
Cash used in financing activities	(64,063)	(69,498)	(32,766)
Foreign currency exchange impact on cash	13	(360)	(379)
(Decrease)/increase in cash and cash equivalents	(3,948)	517	6,012
Cash and cash equivalents at beginning of year	11,703	11,186	5,174
Cash and cash equivalents at end of year	$ 7,755	$ 11,703	$ 11,186

(continued on next page)

(continued from previous page)

DIGITAL WIDGETS, INC.
CONSOLIDATED STATEMENT OF CASH FLOWS
(in thousands)

	Year ended December 31		
	2004	2003	2002
SUPPLEMENTAL CASH FLOW:			
Cash paid for interest	$ 1,507	$ 2,355	$ 5,978
Cash paid for income taxes	20,980	23,433	39,669
Non-cash financing activities:			
Dividends payable	753	801	—
Treasury stock repurchases payable	—	3,933	—
Merger transactions:			
Fair value of assets acquired	—	6,734	28,987
Fair value of liabilities assumed	—	(1,409)	(10,038)
Cash paid	—	5,325	18,949
Other cash payments related to mergers	2,508	2,652	3,412
Less cash acquired	—	(1,459)	(6,218)
Net cash paid for mergers	$ 2,508	$ 6,518	$16,143

Understand the Culture and Environment

As you are well aware, every corporation has its own style, its own culture, its own structure, its own values and purpose, and its own way of doing business. The more you know about these intangibles, the more you will be able to say the right things at the right time to the right people.

Some key things to learn about the environment are

- Corporate structure: Is it publicly held? An S-corp? A wholly owned subsidiary? How a company is structured will affect how plans are executed, where decisions are made, and who allocates the money to fund solutions.

- Organizational structure—corporate hierarchy/reporting relationships: What is the chain of command? Who reports to whom? How are decisions made? What is the flow of communications?

- Corporate decision makers and influencers: How and where are decisions made, and who influences those decisions?

ANALYZE

No surprise here: analysis is the logical next step. You've collected lots of information. Now you've got to figure out what it means and how to apply it to your positioning theme, value proposition, and sales effort. Remember data, dialogue, and discipline? Well, you've got the data, and now you need the discipline to do a comprehensive and thorough analysis to enrich the dialogue you will have with the customer.

Part of your analysis should be to look at the numbers. You should also thoroughly understand or try to project how your customer will use your solution. Does your solution help your prospective customer, and ideally your customer's customer, improve financial performance? Knowledge of both these areas is critical to your ability to successfully sell a business solution to your prospect.

Understand Financial Ratios

The easiest way to understand a company's financial statements is to perform a few basic—but highly revealing—ratio calculations. Simple ratios, like the ones I describe below, go a long way towards helping you evaluate the true financial state of your prospect.

Profitability Ratios If you understand key performance ratios you can use them as a benchmark to compare against your prospect's industry and competitors' data. Then use your insight to target high-ranking decision makers. Remember, a single ratio on its own is of very little value. Ratios need to be analyzed compared with industry norms and past corporate performance.

Activity Ratios Activity ratios measure productivity and indicate how effectively a company is using its resources. Included in major activity ratios are

- Receivables turnover: Net sales/Average trade receivables (net); measures liquidity of receivables

- Inventory turnover: Cost of goods sold/Average inventory; measures liquidity of inventory

- Asset turnover: Net sales/Average total assets; measures how effectively assets are used to create sales

---

Ratios 101

When analyzing ratios, keep this in mind: Balance sheet information represents a point in time. Income statement information shows data for a period of time. Therefore, if you are examining ratios that involve numbers from both the balance sheet and the income statement, make sure that the data point you use from the balance sheet is an average—from two balance sheets representing the two points in time reflected on the income statement.

Liquidity Ratios Liquidity ratios indicate a company's liquidity and tell you if they can pay their maturing obligations. Some key liquidity ratios include:

- Current ratio: Current assets/Current liabilities; measures the company's ability to pay short-term debt

- Quick or Acid Test ratio: Cash, marketable securities, and accounts receivable (Net)/Current liabilities; measures immediate short-term liquidity

Coverage Ratios

Coverage ratios are used to test the adequacy of cash flows generated through earnings for purposes of meeting debt and lease obligations, including the interest coverage ratio and the fixed-charge coverage ratio.

FIGURE A-7   *Understanding profitability ratios*

If you understand your prospect's profitability ratios	You can build an "executive" conversation
Return on Sales (ROS; net profit divided by revenues [sales]) *A reduction of ROS can mean the sales force is selling smaller orders, discounting more, or changing the product mix to a less profitable group of products.*	Talk about discounting, selling smaller orders, or cost areas that may be growing too quickly. Expand the conversation to include the difficulties of getting new products to market and making higher margins.
Return on Net Assets (net profit divided by average total assets) *If this ratio is in decline, it may mean that the company is making lower margin on its assets.*	Talk about how your company's product or solution can help optimize the use of assets.
Return on Equity (ROE; net income divided by average shareholder equity) *A measure of how the company has produced a profit using its investors' money (their equity).*	Talk about how investing in your solution will cause their net income (after deducting the cost of your solution) to be significantly greater than if they did not, thus significantly increasing their ROE. Beware: If your target company has a highly leveraged capital structure (low equity, high debt), then ROE may not be an important consideration compared to other financial measures.
Gross Profit Margin (revenues less cost of goods sold divided by revenues) *This ratio shows the effects of rising production costs or discounting on the organization's products. Gross profit percentage declines when costs of products are rising faster than sales.*	If there is a reduction in gross margin, talk about your client company's ability to gain better pricing on its products using your solution.
Net Profit Margin (net profit divided by sales) *This is an important bottom-line measurement—especially when you are looking at a business that has very little in the way of cost of goods sold.*	Talk about how the net operating profit on your investment after the cost of it is going to increase profits (assuming the cost of your solution is fully expensed as opposed to capitalizing it).

Coverage ratios include:

- Debt to Total Capital: Debt/Debt + equity; measures how much of the balance sheet is financed with debt
- Times Interest Earned: Earnings before interest and taxes / Interest charges; measures a company's ability to meet interest payments as they come due
- Cash Debt Coverage ratio: Funds from operations/Average total debt; measures a company's ability to repay total liabilities from its operations in a given year

Assess the Buyer's Intention

After you're comfortable with the numbers, analyze what you know about the buyer's intentions. You can do this by getting the answers to some basic questions:

- What is the buyer's motivation?
- What business issue(s) does our product solve for the customer?
- Do they have a sense of urgency about solving their business issues?
- Specifically, what operational improvements or financial results will our product provide our customer?
- What do they expect in return or as "payback" if they choose us as the vendor?
- Given their business issue(s), what are the consequences of taking action? Of not taking action?
- Do they have the resources or means to act? Or is the purchase contingent on factors that are pending, unknown, or not yet quantified?
- What risks does the buyer perceive in choosing our solution? What about in not choosing our solution?

APPLY

When you've done your research and you know what drives your customer's business, you will be able to apply that knowledge to position your products or services as part of a strategic solution to the challenges of your customer's business and industry.

Look for Opportunities to Create Value

If you've done a thorough job researching your prospect, you should know

- What your customer's business issues are (i.e., what's keeping him or her awake at night such as strategic challenges or risks that affect financial performance)
- How those issues play out in real dollars (i.e., how they could affect the bottom line)
- How your product or service will help your customer resolve his or her business issues

When you're discerning how you can help your customer resolve a business issue, think multidimensionally. Your solution can (and should) have a positive impact at several levels. You should be able to answer these questions for your prospective or existing customers:

- What is the corporate impact of applying your product or solution in their organization?
- What is the financial performance impact?
    - What is the revenue impact? How will your solution help your customers increase their revenue by customer and capture new customers?
    - What is the cost reduction impact? How will your solution help reduce or contain costs?
    - How will your business solution help your customer become more profitable and lead to increased shareholder value?

- What is the productivity impact? How does your solution positively or negatively affect your customer's employees? Does it increase productivity? Improve morale?

- What is the functional impact? How will your business solution improve productivity within and between your customer's departments? Will it improve efficiency? Streamline processes? Reduce risk? Increase responsiveness?

Once you are able to define your product's impact, you should be able to identify the costs and benefits of your product or service for your customer. You can then start formulating the positioning of your value proposition, which you can communicate to your customer. This will have far greater value to your prospect than simply discussing features, benefits, and price.

Frame Your Value Proposition

People talk about the value proposition a lot these days. Have you ever wondered just exactly what a value proposition is? Broadly speaking, it is a statement or theme that describes how your product or service is going to help your prospect solve a business problem, provide an opportunity, or realize some economic benefit.

Winning value propositions are comprised of five components and delivered in language that executives speak and understand.

The components are

- What you propose to do: save time, save money, provide a solution, provide an opportunity, provide value, and so on

- How you propose to do it: what it will take, what's required of you, what's required of the prospect

- What it will cost: actual, range, and other estimates depending on circumstances

- Your forecast: what the client will save, generate in revenue, and potentially realize in return on investment (ROI)

- A promise: to track actual ROI or in some way demonstrate that the value proposed will actually be received

EXECUTIVE LANGUAGE

To craft an effective sales presentation, you will need to frame your value proposition using terminology and language that demonstrates that you understand and empathize with the prospect's point of view.

To do this, you must learn to speak in the vernacular used by finance, operations, sales, IT, and executive management, and articulate a potential solution in terms of the business value to the client.

A value proposition that incorporates the essential elements above and speaks to executives in their own language might look something like this: "Our solution set will increase the overall quality of your manufacturing process and dramatically increase customer satisfaction. The solution will require ongoing commitment from senior management to reinforce the new processes institutionalized in the organization. Your overall investment is less than one quarter of a percentage point of the return on investment that you will receive as a result of embedding our solution. Specifically, you should realize a minimum of 5 percent revenue and margin lift (which we will measure using your systems and metrics) as a result of using our solution, not to mention realizing a significant increase in customer satisfaction and goodwill." (Make sure your value proposition can be backed up with data.)

EXECUTE

As you hone your business acumen skills, you will find that you will be in position to use *The Last Link* toolkit—Pivotal Agreements; the 3D Model—data, dialogue, and discipline; Sales Execution Plans; and the Dialogue Principles—as you execute your own company's strategy at the customer interface.

Your enhanced business acumen will enable you to build credibility and develop relationships based on trust and respect at higher levels in customer organizations—where strategic selling is most fruitful, with the real decision makers.

COURSE B

The Change Factor

To implement the tools of *The Last Link* in your organization, you must be able to manage a change process. In my experience, successful change programs begin with results. That means focusing change efforts on results-oriented rather than activity-oriented efforts. The 3D Model is a results-oriented process that allows leaders to bypass lengthy preparation and aim for quick, measurable strategic gains at the customer interface.

This course contains a brief but comprehensive review of several winning change management principles. Change must be managed, and that means that senior-level executives must be clear on what they are trying to achieve and willing to stay the course. As you create your strategic plans, make sure you review these change management principles and factor them into your planning, communications, management systems, and processes, and apply them to implementing results-oriented methodologies like the 3D Model.

PRINCIPLES OF SUCCESSFUL CHANGE

Because the path to success is often rocky and fraught with unforeseen challenges, people often give up on change before they achieve the results they seek. Change sticks when the components of the change become norms, "the way we do things around here." Don't confuse the appearance of change with the reality of change. If you execute your change strategy with the following principles in mind, you'll avoid many of the mistakes most organizations make and be in a position to implement the lessons of *The Last Link* effectively.

Create a Sense of Urgency

Have you ever noticed what happens when a fire alarm goes off? People immediately begin to move with a sense of urgency; their senses are heightened, their adrenaline starts pumping, and they are suddenly focused on the business of survival.

Now, I'm not suggesting that you run your change management process like a fire drill. But I am suggesting that when you are trying to manage change you need to be intentional and create a sense of urgency. This shouldn't be hard to do. In today's business climate there is always a challenge, a change, or even a crisis that requires focused attention. Externally, you just have to look at your company's competitive situation, market position, technological trends, and financial performance. Internally, look at the company's structure, reporting relationships, discipline, work ethic, and the gap between having a strategy and executing it. Any of these factors can represent a threat to your ability to survive and grow.

A lot of companies develop a sense of urgency because they are in pain: their profits are down, their competitors are beating them up in the marketplace, technology is making their product or service offerings obsolete, or they are not executing their corporate strategy at the customer inter-face. This kind of pain can be highly motivating and unquestionably cre-ates a sense of urgency: business as usual is no longer an option and the unknown—change—is a better bet than the status quo.

Pressure and urgency are useful change agents. Use them to your advantage.

Form a Change Coalition

If you are going to manage meaningful change, you need to form a change coalition. To do this, you need to assemble a critical mass of stakehold-ers—twenty to fifty people—and develop among the coalition a shared assessment of the company's problems and opportunities. The members of the change coalition must share some minimum level of trust and com-munication among themselves.

So that begs the question—who do you pick to be a part of this change coalition? Obviously you want to retain those trusted advisors and team members with power. And of course power comes in many forms: the power of title, the power of information and expertise, the power of repu-tation, the power of relationships.

There is another interesting factor to consider. Remember the bell-shaped marketing curve (fig. B-1). It postulates that acceptance, whether it is embracing a new product or a new way of doing business, occurs quickly for some and takes longer for others.

Innovators, early adopters, early majority, late majority, laggards: they all embrace products or—for purposes of our discussion—accept change at different rates. When you form your change coalition, consider this fac-tor: whether you're an older company in extreme pain where everyone has given up on the tried and true methods that used to work but don't any-more, or a young, growing company where workflow methods are working, revisiting workflow processes and procedures in a proactive way is healthy. Change is a reality of any business or relationship and it is an essential ele-ment for sustained growth.

FIGURE B-1   *The marketing bell curve applies to change management.*

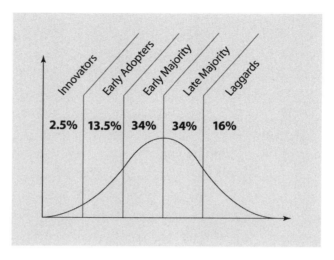

Face the Pain

Generally change occurs only after there is an honest recognition of pain. Before you can acknowledge pain, you have to take a hard look at reality. In many organizations this is not easy to do. Too often there is an unspoken rule that managers don't want to hear the truth, they just want to hear what they want to hear.

In this kind of environment it is difficult to take a stab at revitalization because it means facing pain, and that means admitting that you're not doing some critical things right. It also means taking risks, probing for the truth, and listening to ideas and opinions you might not like.

Any change process must begin with an honest appraisal of what you're doing well and what you're not doing well. In my experience, most organizations that are failing to meet their numbers don't plan effectively, don't use the right tools, and don't do a good job of communicating, coaching, setting expectations, and holding people accountable.

When this is the case, poor performance must be acknowledged with a resolve to do things differently and better for the scene to be set for change. Facing the pain is a critical step in the process of change management.

Visualize the Future and Articulate It (in Less than Five Minutes)

By facing the pain you can develop a keen understanding of where things are veering off track and going wrong. From a state of deep understanding of current reality, you can begin to envision the future of what the desired state of high performance should look like.

Use your change coalition to develop a vision of the future that clarifies the direction in which your company needs to move. Stay focused only on results-oriented projects, methods, and disciplines that will achieve the vision.

Make your plan brief and to the point. Remember this rule of thumb: If you can't communicate the vision to someone in five minutes or less and get a reaction that signifies both understanding and interest, you need to go back and refine the vision until it sparks a connection with the team.

When charts and diagrams are unable to capture the complexity of concepts and motivate the people in your organization, a simple story is always effective in clarifying the concept. Cautionary tales, success stories, and innovative approaches used by others can all be catalysts for forward movement.

Know the Opposition

Things are not going to happen without strong line leadership. Know your opposition. Don't let the opposition stop the change. Harness their contentious energy instead. Keep in touch; know their issues; keep dialogue open; test assumptions; find ways to team up with them and focus on the higher business purpose. Neutralize their negative charge by getting them to work on things that they believe in and care about that ultimately can lead to the better solution.

Know Why Employees Resist Change

Resistance. Entropy. These are common phenomena in large (and even small) corporations today. Resistance can be passive or active, but either way, it's the kiss of death to a change movement. It leads to entropy and the maintenance of the status quo.

In an urgent situation, where change is necessary to prosper and in many cases just to survive, resistance slows you down and often brings positive change to a screeching halt. There will always be resistance to change—no matter what the company is, who the players are, or what the change is. The trick is to anticipate resistance, plan for it, and manage it proactively.

Don't ignore resistance. Don't try to overpower it. Seek it out; meet it halfway; bring it out into the open. Facilitate open discussion where resistance can be turned into constructive criticism. If resistance goes underground, it is difficult to fight. But resistance that is articulated, that has a face and an agenda, can be fashioned to build stronger and more diverse change coalitions.

Resistors have valuable perspectives and points of view. Let their views inform how you manage change and the pace at which it goes.

Expand Your Base

Change starts small. Innovators are the first to change, followed by "early adopters," followed by the "early majority," and so on. Plan to leverage the natural course of change adoption by deepening and expanding your base as change starts to happen. Involve more and more people as the process progresses. And be sure to keep picking the right people—the ones who want to change; who "get it" and who can take the proverbial ball and run with it; who have the respect and admiration of others.

Empower People to Do the Right Thing

Most people are hard-wired to do the right things if conditions are right. But there has to be trust, safety, and incentive. To engender this kind of environment, make sure your goals and methods are transparent enough that your employees will be willing to take some calculated risks.

Remove Obstacles

Make it easy for people to change. Often, when you're introducing change, there are obstacles that represent barriers to success. Sometimes these obstacles are real and sometimes they are in people's heads.

Real obstacles are things like old-line managers who don't embrace change and aren't managing to achieve the change results; an organizational hierarchy that doesn't allow cooperation between critical entities (like corporate development, marketing, sales, and production); or a laissez-faire culture that doesn't embrace discipline or enforce a work ethic. These are real obstacles, but not insurmountable obstacles. Company managers with insight and will can make corrections as they perform and learn, and can eventually remove these obstacles.

Obstacles in people's heads are no less important, but require a different approach to change management. A "You can't get there from here" mentality can often be changed through team building, coaching, holding people accountable, and providing the right incentives. By the same token, don't be afraid to remove people who aren't willing or can't seem to adhere to new standards.

Encourage Managers to See for Themselves

Don't force people to take your word for it. Encourage managers, influencers, and key performers to see for themselves.

Put these people on the forefront of the change experience. Give them training. Have them apply the principles of *The Last Link* in their own unit, department, or division. Let them take the leap and see if they get the results you are predicting today, tomorrow, in the next week, or next month or two. I have seen countless people pick up new skills in a class on the Dialogue Principles, apply them in a real sales situation during a break, and show immediate results. People are far more likely to change their behavior when they have proven to themselves that the new method works. When you isolate the successes and share them with your people, you can create a domino effect and motivate others in the organization to follow suit.

Overcommunicate

Overcommunicate and use all appropriate communications vehicles frequently. The need for change has to be stated often and consistently. Use every possible channel, especially those that are being wasted on nonessential information. Make your messages interesting and provocative. Establish communication venues that give people a place to be creative and a chance to be heard. Remember: an effective message changes the receiver's knowledge, attitude, and behavior.

Help people see the connections between change, behavior, and success through good communication. Don't let people make the wrong conclusions about why something works. Otherwise, left to their own devices, they might very well do the wrong thing. Performance appraisals are a great opportunity to talk about how the employee's behavior helps or undermines the vision.

GET THE CHANGE FUNDAMENTALS RIGHT

Underpinning all the change management principles I've articulated above are what I call the fundamentals of change. These are nonnegotiables that you must get right for real change to occur.

Walk the Talk

Leaders must behave in ways that reflect what they are saying. Nothing undermines change more than behavior by important individuals that is inconsistent with their words.

Change requires short-term sacrifice. Employees won't engage in short-term sacrifice unless they believe that change is possible. How do you communicate that change is possible? By behaving in ways that reflect what you are saying.

Don't Declare Victory too Early

"In the final analysis," writes John P. Kotter, professor of leadership at Harvard Business School, "change sticks when it becomes 'the way we do things around here' . . . Until new behaviors are rooted in social norms and shared values, they are always subject to degradation as soon as the pressures associated with a change effort are removed."[1]

Educate yourself on what the change process entails. Knowing what to expect and how to navigate the troubled waters of any change process will prepare you for hanging in there over the long haul.

Declaring victory too early kills an initiative that hasn't been fully integrated into the company culture. Rather than declaring victory, use the credibility short-term wins create to tackle even bigger problems.

Plan for and Create Short-term Wins

Results get results, and nothing succeeds like success. Success fuels motivation and can create a friendly competition among peers that spurs each individual on to greater performance.

Plan for change over the long-term, but plot the course of the desired change to incorporate frequent, short-term interim wins. Small but frequent wins solidify resolve and keep teams motivated. "Bite-size" goals can be achieved with some dispatch and keep everybody focused and hopeful.

Look for win opportunities and shape performance to gain those wins. That means establishing goals in the yearly planning process, looking for ways to obtain clear performance improvements, rewarding those who achieve the objectives, and coaching or removing those who don't. Remember to communicate wins early and often.

Rewards don't have to be just money (in fact, there are studies that indicate that offering financial rewards can occasionally be counterproductive). Reward your people with recognition and even promotions.

Periodically review strategy, and learn from both success and failures. Institutionalize the changes that work and get rid of the rest. Change requires some degree of risk taking, but it is an inevitable part of every business and relationship. If you are not changing, you are dying.

COURSE C

Reality Selling

By now you have developed an in-depth understanding of the concepts I explain in the book. In this section, you have the opportunity to put your new knowledge to the test.

This case study uses a fictional Fortune 200 global company—Digital Widgets, Inc.—that manufactures high-tech widgets at facilities around the world. The case materials include a three-act play that tells the story of management woes and sales challenges during a typical quarter at Digital Widgets, Inc., and a complete set of financials for the company.

If you feel ready, read the story, study the financials, and then answer the questions on page 184 to test your corporate strategy execution knowledge as well as your business acumen skills.

ACT I

SCENE I: The Heat Is On

Present time. Digital Widgets, Inc., headquarters, 33rd floor, Anytown, USA, 6:30 AM. EVP of Sales, Joe Moreno, just back in the office after a four-day cross-country trip, spots an interesting item on the Wall Street Journal *website.*

High-tech widgets in the news: *Jonathan Smith, CEO of Tetra Widgets, announced that the company has developed a new robotic manufacturing system that will lead to a drop in prices. "The products that high-tech widgets are used in—computers, cell phones, and consumer electronics—are expected to have unprecedented growth. Industry leaders like my company realized that the name of the game is gaining economies of scale and moving down the experience curve fast enough to keep ahead of rapidly lowering unit prices. Companies that can't keep up won't survive."* (*Article on page 32*)

Joe (thinking to himself): I wonder how the Blue Moon deal is going.

SCENE II: Parachuting the CEO in for the Big Deal

The same morning, 600 miles away—southern region, state capital.
    CEO Robert Brentwood of Digital Widgets, Inc., has "parachuted in" to help close a critical piece of business with an important customer: Blue Moon Electronics. Robert and the regional sales crew—Bill, Digital's southern region manager, and Marlene, Digital's large business sales rep for the Blue Moon account—are huddled around a table at a local restaurant.

Robert: So, what's the status of the Blue Moon account and what do we need to accomplish today?

Bill: We're competing with Tetra Widgets, and Blue Moon is putting the heat on us to make some concessions. They're looking for an extra ten points on the price and some pretty onerous terms and conditions. Our legal people have talked and we've worked out the T&Cs, but the price thing is still an issue.

Marlene: We're trying to close this deal by the end of the quarter, so we arranged a meeting with their top people to move things along. We wanted you here to demonstrate Digital Widgets' commitment to

Blue Moon and to make sure that they understand what an important customer they are to us.

Robert: All right, so who's going to be in the meeting?

Robert pulls out a small black notebook and gold pen. Bill grabs a napkin and draws a quick chart of who's who.

Bill: We've been dealing with one of the procurement managers and the operations managers, but the CEO, Henry Lewis, will be in the meeting this morning.

Robert makes notes as Bill talks.

Robert (confidently): Got it, let's go.

Later that morning, Blue Moon headquarters. Blue Moon's CEO, Henry Lewis, along with a couple of unexpected players—Blue Moon's head of product development, the operations team lead, and the chief procurement officer—introduce themselves to the Digital Widgets team.

Henry (affably): Bill and Marlene have told me you're not going to lose any business to Tetra, or any other competitors, due to lack of flexibility on pricing.

Robert: Henry, we pride ourselves on being responsive to important customers like Blue Moon; we're here today to make sure you know that.

SCENE III: The Tough Conversation on the Ninth Hole

The following weekend, second month of the quarter, ninth hole, Garden Valley Golf Club. Robert, Joe, and Helen (Digital Widgets' CFO) are working their way up the fairway. Joe takes two more shots to get his ball in the hole.

Robert: Let's see . . . that's four for me; five for Helen, and Joe . . . mmm . . . seven, that's three over par. Joe, I hope our quarterly numbers are better than your golf score.

Helen (worried): I just saw the month-end numbers and they're not looking good.

Robert: Let's hear it.

Helen: We've picked up market share but our margins are so low we're going to have to cut some more cost out of the operation to cover our overhead if we can't turn this around.

Robert: Joe, I don't get it. What's going on? Why are our margins taking such a nosedive?

Joe: Well, the costs of sale continue to increase . . . and there are a number of things we're trying to put in place off the work with the McKinsey study around price management and margin control that haven't gotten traction yet. We're still getting uneven results across our sales regions on pricing and margins.

Robert: At this rate, our numbers are going to be worse than last quarter's! We're really going to have to make a big point at the next analysts' call about the initiatives we're putting in place to turn these numbers around. Let's nail this down at next week's meeting with Arthur.

SCENE IV: What Do Our Experts Have to Say About This?

Quarter end, Digital Widgets, Inc. boardroom. Arthur Hamilton, senior partner at McKinsey & Company, responds to Robert's concern about the sagging numbers and the upcoming analysts' call.

Arthur: Robert, I couldn't agree with you more. Given the poor performance for this quarter, it would be a good idea to raise the visibility of the pricing management and margin erosion initiatives at the next analysts' call. The challenge you have, Robert, is that based on the most recent numbers we've analyzed, the problem has gotten worse—not better—on both the pricing and margin fronts. We recommend a four-step plan for turning things around. One, improve the consistency of the application of new pricing software across all regions. Two, focus on minimizing post-sale margin erosion. Three, improve Digital Widgets' ability to negotiate more profitably with customer procurement and sourcing officers. And, four, leverage the new CRM system more effectively. We think that if you focus on this four-pronged strategy for making things happen you're going to be able to move the numbers.

Joe: I absolutely agree with Arthur. And I think we're on it. We're redoubling our current efforts to make sure the CRM pricing software and margin management initiatives work consistently across our territories; we're making major strides across the northeast; and frankly, considering the energy we've put into the launching of the Digital Widgets 2010, it doesn't surprise me that it's taking a little more time to get some of these things taken care of.

Robert: I understand what you're saying, Joe. OK, I think we've got a plan for the analysts' meeting next week. Arthur, why don't you finish up your report and we'll get together one more time to go over your recommendations before the call.

SCENE V: This CRM Software Should Help

The following day, Digital Widgets, Inc., technology center. CRM Project Manager Harold Wang gives the CRM Project Oversight Group a status on the project.

Harold: Joe, we're not getting the compliance we need from the sales team on the use of the CRM system.

Joe: We're working on it, Harold. But I'm getting feedback from the field that it's increased their administrative work and they are not getting a lot back that helps them sell better. And some of the older dogs on the sales force haven't gotten comfortable with using the new technology; we're working on that too.

Harold: That makes sense to me, Joe. You'll recall our main mission with the CRM system was to provide data to management to help them manage their sales force better; you can always expect to get that kind of feedback from the field.

Joe: By the way, I'm looking at your report, Harold. What's the status on getting the margin module into the system? You know Robert's really beating the drum on margin management. It seems to me that it's critical to have that up and running as soon as possible.

Harold gives a quick glance at his boss, CIO Charlotte Newman. She nods; they knew this question was coming.

Harold: As you can see it's in the queue. It's complicated. We're trying to line up the priorities of the finance people and manage a number of the other IT priorities we've been given. These things just take time. We've had some issues in alpha testing . . . it's the nature of the beast. This is complicated, as you know, and it's going to take us a while to work things out.

Charlotte: Joe, we're juggling a lot of priorities. Who could have predicted we'd be hit with Sarbanes Oxley? But let me assure you, we're analyzing resources and looking at making some new hires.

Joe: I understand. Nevertheless, this is really important. See what you can do. Can we get an update at the next meeting?

Joe (thinks to himself): Wow, $21 million, eleven months late, and this is all we've got to show?

ACT II

SCENE I: OmniCor Wants Us to Bid on the RFP (Request for Proposal)

One week later, Digital Widgets, Inc., northwest regional office. EVP of Sales Joe Moreno is onsite. His regional sales manager, Ellie Young, briefs him on a new opportunity.

Ellie: First the good news: OmniCor's sales are going through the roof and they need to expand their supply to keep up with demand. Clearly this is a good opportunity for us to expand our business. Now the bad news: they're going with an RFP process, and they're inviting us to bid on the business.

Joe: Did you know about the RFP?

Ellie: No, Pete just found out ... evidently OmniCor is reevaluating their whole widget-purchasing program, so they're doing this bid by the books.

Joe (thinks to himself): An RFP ... when a bid like this goes out to RFP, some other vendor has most likely shaped the specs and our chances of winning the business go down.

Ellie: We're committed to winning the business, but we could be in for a rough ride here based on stuff that's happening with the account.

Joe: Do what you have to do to put a bid together. Make sure you stay on top of it.

SCENE II: Meanwhile, over at OmniCor Headquarters

The same afternoon, OmniCor headquarters. VP of Manufacturing Mark Stancioff and Purchasing Manager Louise Dulles are strategizing on how to handle the widget bidding process.

Mark: Here are the constraints we are working under: You know we've got to reduce costs. But it's expensive to qualify a new vendor. So I'd just as soon go with Digital Widgets. We have already integrated their delivery system into our supply chain. And I'm not eager to switch over to a new widget, even if we can get it more cheaply. From a total-cost-of-ownership perspective, the only reason to switch vendors is if we can get a dramatically lower price.

Louise: OK, anything else?

Mark: Oh, another reason to keep Digital Widgets around. Given their manufacturing locations, they can provide more reliable supply and better service to our plants in Europe and Asia than their major competitors.

Louise: Sounds like Digital Widgets has the inside track on this, all things considered. But we're definitely going to squeeze them on price!

Mark: Can you pull it off?

Louise: I'll do my best.

SCENE III: The Quarterly Analysts' Call

The following Thursday, Digital Widgets, Inc., boardroom, during a teleconference with Wall Street analysts. Fifteen minutes into the call, after the disappointing nature of the financial results becomes clear, the gloves come off.

Ben: Ben Walters here, Morgan Stanley. Let me net out what I'm hearing. In spite of your new product launch, your growth just isn't keeping up with your peer group, your costs are increasing, and your margins are shrinking. Looks like your corporate strategy isn't producing the results you're looking for. What's your strategy for turning this around?

Robert: Ben, we're addressing the situation with a four-pronged strategy. We're working on improving consistency of application of our new pricing software across all regions. We're focusing on minimizing postsale margin erosion; we're putting a new seven-step process in place to improve Digital Widgets' sales professionals' ability to negotiate more profitably with customer procurement and sourcing officers. And finally, we're working hard to leverage our new CRM system more effectively.

Sally: Sally Jenkins at Bear Stearns . . . With your price–earnings ratio north of fifty, any hiccup in your numbers could really hammer your stock price. How confident are you that you can execute?

Robert: We're confident our team can turn this around.

SCENE IV: The New Corporate Strategy Is Unveiled

Midquarter, one month after the analysts' call, Grand Hotel Ballroom, Anytown, USA.

The lights dim. Several notes blast from the sound system before everyone recognizes the theme to Rocky *and cheers. Projected onto the three screens that frame the podium are images of Lance Armstrong cycling up the Champs Elysée with Team America. Flash to Tiger Woods sinking a putt with his patented clenched fist. Flash to the Boston Red Sox rushing onto the field after winning the 2004 World Series. The narrator talks about courage, determination, and teamwork.*

The video finishes and the spotlight settles onto Digital Widgets' CEO, Robert Brentwood. He surveys the entire Digital sales team seated in the elegant Grand Hotel Ballroom.

Robert (stoked): I am so proud to be here with you today. You are the people who make all this possible. You are the front line. You are the best sales force in our industry and together we will lead the growth of our company into the future.

Cheers and whistles erupt throughout the ballroom.

Robert: You all know why you're here . . .

A slide flashes onto all three screens: Digital Widgets Corporate Strategy Launch: "Whatever It Takes"

Robert: We're here to do whatever it takes to bring in sales!

Robert talks through a thirty-slide PowerPoint presentation and makes his concluding remarks.

Robert: This is important to Digital Widgets and this is important to you. That's why we're investing in a four-pronged strategy: leveraging the new pricing software, minimizing postsale margin erosion, improving our ability to negotiate more profitably, and leveraging our new CRM more effectively . . .

Robert jabs both fists into the air and bellows.

Robert: Together, we will do whatever it takes to win business and increase sales!

The sales team rises to their feet, applauding and chanting.

Audience: Whatever it takes! Whatever it takes! Whatever it takes!

There is a buzz of excitement in the air as the room clears and people meander off for the mid-morning break. EVP of Sales Joe Moreno chats up various salespeople. And then suddenly he is alone in the room.

Joe (thinks to himself): Well, the bar has definitely been raised. Great strategy . . . Now what?

SCENE V: Getting Ready for the Final OmniCor Presentation

Ten days later, at the Digital Widgets, Inc., regional office in the northeast. Digital Regional Sales Manager Ellie Young meets with Sales Representative Amy King to go over tomorrow's presentation of their request for proposal response to OmniCor.

Ellie: This RFP sure doesn't give us a chance to position our value, does it? By the way, what happened when you talked to Burt at Omni-Cor about how we could leverage our existing work to improve our response to the RFP?

Amy: I wasn't able to connect; I got a voice mail back from them referring me back to the purchasing people. Boy, things really got different after they put the RFP in place. I'm totally locked out.

Ellie (resigned):   So, we are where we are. All right then, let's look at the PowerPoint presentation we're going to use tomorrow. What's the strategy?

Ellie flips through her hard copy of the presentation; Amy notices it is heavily annotated.

Ellie (determined):   There are some things we need to change.

Amy looks at her watch. It's already after six. She wonders if she'll get dinner tonight.

SCENE VI: The Final Negotiation with Purchasing at OmniCor

One week later, OmniCor headquarters. Digital Sales Manager Ellie Young and Sales Representative Amy King meet with OmniCor Purchasing Manager Louise Dulles and the VP of Manufacturing, Mark Stancioff.

Louise: We liked your proposal, and, as I told you on the phone, we've selected you to be the vendor.

Ellie: We're very pleased to have this opportunity to continue to deepen our relationship.

Louise: When we notified you that you won the bid, we thought you had a better deal. Actually, on further analysis, that didn't turn out to be the case. We liked your proposal, but we called you in today because we need your best and final price.

They haggle over several items.

Ellie: If I do that for you, is that going to work?

Louise: Yes, that will do it.

Ellie excuses herself to make a phone call. She returns five minutes later.

Ellie: You've got a deal.

ACT III

SCENE I: What's Happening with the Blue Moon Deal?

Early evening, later that day, Digital Widgets, Inc., headquarters. CEO Robert Brentwood pops in on EVP of Sales Joe Moreno unexpectedly.

Robert: So, what's happening with the Blue Moon deal? Are there any new developments?

Joe: We haven't been able to close it yet; in fact, we had to go back and reprice the deal.

Robert: We're going to reprice the deal even after I already gave them a price?

Joe: We didn't have a choice. Tetra Widgets came back to them with an even better price than we expected and—given the importance of market share at this point—we're trying to figure out how we can match it. Of course, that's slowed down the sales cycle. And put us in a situation that has caused an internal dispute, trying to figure out which division is going to take the hit on the additional discounts. I'm meeting with financing tomorrow to try and resolve it. Frankly, I don't see this closing by end of quarter.

SCENE II: Did We Make Our Margins on OmniCor?

The next day, Joe's office. Joe discusses the OmniCor deal with Ellie.

Ellie: We got the deal, but the pricing is bare bones and we had to make a number of concessions. As you know, we weren't comfortable doing that as they weren't complying with their current annual volume commitment. And then they had the nerve to ask for even more free service with the new contract! We felt the only way to close the deal was to give in.

Joe: What about the custom packaging issue?

Ellie (sheepishly): Oh, that was the other problem. It turns out that Omni-Cor called their contacts in our manufacturing group to plead their case. I couldn't believe it! Our ops guys told them it was no big deal, so while we're out there positioning custom packaging as expensive and high value, we find out that our technicians are giving it away. And they think they're helping us!

Joe: This isn't right. We had a small amount of business and we were given an opportunity to get a lot more business and we let things get out of control. We obviously blew this thing. We may get some revenue on the books, but we're sure not going to make any money on it.

Ellie: Hey, it's tough to establish value when the buyer sends out an RFP and runs a bidding contest like we're selling a bunch of commodities.

Joe: We've got to be able to do better than this . . .

Joe ends the call and picks up the McKinsey report. He pages through it carefully before tossing it aside.

SCENE III: The Blue Moon Deal: "We Tanked"

One week later, early morning. Joe checks e-mail and plans his day. The phone rings. It's Bill, Digital's southern region sales manager.

Bill: The Blue Moon deal . . . I just got word. We tanked.

Joe: What the hell went wrong, Bill? You said all the buying signs were right.

Bill: I know, Joe. But they ran an end-around at the last minute. We think they were playing us against Tetra Widgets. They were working us . . .

Joe: . . . and we're just now finding out?

Joe's stomach tightens as he glances out his window.

Joe (thinks to himself): So much for the seven-step sales process.

Joe's cell phone rings.

Joe: Bill, we'll have to debrief later, Robert's calling.

Robert: Joe, I just heard we didn't get the business I parachuted in on. What was it called? Blue Moon? Ha! How ironic. Listen, we need to understand in detail what went on here and how we can avoid it in the future.

Joe: I was just talking to Bill, trying to get the full story.

Robert: Look, Joe, if we can't link strategy to sales, we're going to be executed. Find out where we missed the boat and get back to me. I want to know exactly what happened. I'll need a full report next Monday for Tuesday's management meeting.

EPILOGUE

Early afternoon, Digital Widgets, Inc., headquarters. EVP of Sales Joe Moreno hangs up the phone. For the past two days he has been investigating what went wrong on the Blue Moon deal. And because the OmniCor deal was on his radar screen—he's still fuming about the low margins they got—he's done a thorough account review on that deal as well. He starts to write his report—which is sure to be grist for the mill at tomorrow's management meeting.

DIGITAL WIDGETS, INC.
BACKGROUND FINANCIAL INFORMATION

Now that you've read the story, take some time to review the comprehensive financial statements that I have provided. If necessary, review the financial concepts I explained in course A—especially the section on ratios. Then, analyze the balance sheet, income statements, and statement of cash flows, and run a few key ratios.

Try to draw as many conclusions as possible from reviewing and analyzing the financial statements, and then answer the questions that begin on page 184. (Note: The answer key to the questions begins on page 185.)

Good luck!

DIGITAL WIDGETS, INC.
CONSOLIDATED BALANCE SHEETS
(in thousands, except share and per share amounts)

	December 31 2004	December 31 2003
ASSETS		
Current assets:		
Cash and cash equivalents	$ 7,755	$ 11,703
Accounts receivable, net of allowance for doubtful accounts of $8,688 and $9,758 respectively	81,003	83,553
Inventories, net of allowance for reserves of $4,033 and $3,318 respectively	33,468	33,373
Costs and estimated earnings in excess of billings on uncompleted contracts	11,469	15,218
Deferred tax asset	3,443	4,521
Other current assets	8,008	8,856
Total current assets	$145,146	$157,224
Property, plant and equipment, net	24,391	28,948
Goodwill, net	317,308	308,158
Intangibles, net	24,622	24,591
Other assets	2,108	3,356
Total assets	$513,575	$522,277

(continued on next page)

(continued from previous page)

DIGITAL WIDGETS, INC.
CONSOLIDATED BALANCE SHEETS
(in thousands, except share and per share amounts)

	December 31	
	2004	2003
LIABILITIES AND STOCKHOLDERS' EQUITY		
Current liabilities:		
Current debt	$ 884	$ 772
Accounts payable	25,591	25,423
Billings in excess of costs and estimated earnings on uncompleted contracts	4,721	2,746
Accrued compensation and benefits	5,697	5,717
Accrued restructuring expenses	494	5,151
Other accrued expenses	13,488	16,137
Accrued income taxes	3,079	2,450
Total current liabilities	$ 53,954	$ 58,396
Long-term debt	29,314	41,211
Deferred taxes	9,208	10,228
Other liabilities	345	423
Stockholders' equity:		
Preferred stock authorized 5,000,000; par value $1.00; none issued and outstanding	—	—
Common stock authorized 100,000,000; par value $.001; issued 19,393,678 and 19,194,034 shares respectively; outstanding 17,859,330 and 18,771,534 shares respectively	19	19
Additional paid-in capital	270,183	246,059
Retained earnings	335,563	299,198
Treasury stock, at cost, 5,534,348 and 3,822,500 shares respectively	(199,904)	(136,289)
Accumulated other comprehensive income	14,893	3,032
Total stockholders' equity	420,753	412,018
Total liabilities and stockholders' equity	$513,575	$522,277

(continued on next page)

(continued from previous page)

DIGITAL WIDGETS, INC.
CONSOLIDATED BALANCE SHEETS
(in thousands, except share and per share amounts)

	December 31	
	2004	2003
LIABILITIES AND STOCKHOLDERS' EQUITY		
Current liabilities:		
Current debt	$ 884	$ 772
Accounts payable	25,591	25,423
Billings in excess of costs and estimated earnings on uncompleted contracts	4,721	2,746
Accrued compensation and benefits	5,697	5,717
Accrued restructuring expenses	494	5,151
Other accrued expenses	13,488	16,137
Accrued income taxes	3,079	2,450
Total current liabilities	$ 53,954	$ 58,396
Long-term debt	29,314	41,211
Deferred taxes	9,208	10,228
Other liabilities	345	423
Stockholders' equity:		
Preferred stock authorized 5,000,000; par value $1.00; none issued and outstanding	—	—
Common stock authorized 100,000,000; par value $.001; issued 19,393,678 and 19,194,034 shares respectively; outstanding 17,859,330 and 18,771,534 shares respectively	19	19
Additional paid-in capital	270,183	246,059
Retained earnings	335,563	299,198
Treasury stock, at cost, 5,534,348 and 3,822,500 shares respectively	(199,904)	(136,289)
Accumulated other comprehensive income	14,893	3,032
Total stockholders' equity	420,753	412,018
Total liabilities and stockholders' equity	$513,575	$522,277

DIGITAL WIDGETS, INC.
CONSOLIDATED STATEMENT OF CASH FLOWS
(in thousands)

	Year ended December 31		
	2004	2003	2002
CASH FLOWS FROM OPERATING ACTIVITIES			
Net income	$ 39,369	$ 40,571	$ 51,702
Adjustments to reconcile net income to cash provided by operating activities:			
Depreciation and amortization	5,638	6,680	6,911
Gain on sale of property	(443)	—	—
Deferred tax provision/(benefit)	1,988	(6,509)	—
Tax benefit from exercised options	(5,658)	(1,518)	(2,198)
Changes in working capital items:			
Accounts receivable, net	6,238	19,259	42,978
Inventories, net	953	6,662	4,753
Other current assets	14,557	23,248	4,740
Accounts payable	302	(5,598)	(34,009)
Accrued compensation and benefits	(36)	(2,191)	(6,733)
Accrued expenses	(3,558)	(8,438)	(460)
Accrued income taxes	1,134	(319)	(9,658)
Other long-term liabilities	1,978	5,301	(1,898)
Cash provided by operating activities	62,462	77,148	56,128
CASH FLOWS FROM INVESTING ACTIVITIES			
Capital expenditures	$(1,394)	$ (1,298)	$ (3,164)
Capital disposals	1,543	1,044	2,338
Merger transactions and prior merger-related payments, net of cash acquired of $0, $1,459, and $7,050 respectively	(2,508)	(6,518)	(16,143)
Cash used in investing activities	(2,359)	(6,772)	(16,969)

(continued on next page)

(continued from previous page)

DIGITAL WIDGETS, INC.
CONSOLIDATED STATEMENT OF CASH FLOWS
(in thousands)

| | Year ended December 31 | | |
	2004	2003	2002
CASH FLOWS FROM FINANCING ACTIVITIES			
Repayment of borrowings	(191,595)	(110,388)	(158,675)
Proceeds from borrowings	179,667	86,458	116,250
Proceeds from the exercise of options	18,466	3,973	9,659
Payment of dividends	(3,053)	(813)	—
Purchase of treasury stock	(67,548)	(48,728)	—
Cash used in financing activities	(64,063)	(69,498)	(32,766)
Foreign currency exchange impact on cash	13	(561)	(379)
(Decrease)/increase in cash and cash equivalents	(3,948)	517	6,012
Cash and cash equivalents at beginning of year	11,703	11,186	5,174
Cash and cash equivalents at end of year	$ 7,755	$ 11,703	$ 11,186
SUPPLEMENTAL CASH FLOW:			
Cash paid for interest	$ 1,507	$ 2,355	$ 5,978
Cash paid for income taxes	20,980	23,433	39,669
Non-cash financing activities:			
Dividends payable	753	801	—
Treasury stock repurchases payable	—	3,933	—
Merger transactions:			
Fair value of assets acquired	—	6,734	28,987
Fair value of liabilities assumed	—	(1,409)	(10,038)
Cash paid	—	5,325	18,948
Other cash payments related to mergers	2,508	2,653	3,412
Less cash acquired	—	(1,459)	(7,050)
Net cash paid for mergers	$ 2,508	$ 6,518	$ 16,143

MERGER NOTES

During fiscal 2004 and 2003, the company paid $2,508 and $2,652 respectively for obligations related to mergers completed in prior periods.

As of March 31, 2004, certain merger agreements provide for contingent payments of up to $1,550. Upon meeting future operating performance goals, goodwill will be adjusted for the amount of the contingent payments.

During fiscal 2003, the company successfully completed three business combinations that have been accounted for using the purchase method of accounting: June 2002, American Gadgets Inc.; July 2002, Gizmos Limited and Gizmos (Spain) Limited; and January 2003, United Contraptions Ltd. The aggregate purchase price of these three business combinations was approximately $3,833 and resulted in goodwill of $2,764 and other intangibles of $290 in accordance with SFAS No. 141, "Business Combinations," which the company adopted during the third quarter of fiscal 2002. The other intangibles balance consisted of noncompete agreements and backlog.

The company has consolidated the results of operations for each of the acquired companies as of the respective merger date. The following table reports pro forma information as if the acquired entities had been purchased at the beginning of the stated periods.

DIGITAL WIDGETS, INC.
MERGER NOTES

		Year ended December 31	
		2004	2003
		(UNAUDITED)	(UNAUDITED)
Revenue	As reported	$433,677	$504,181
	Mergers—pre-Digital Widgets, Inc.	—	2,443
	Pro forma	433,677	506,623
Net income	As reported	$ 39,369	$ 40,571
	percentage of revenues	9.1%	8.0%
	Mergers—pre-Digital Widgets, Inc.	—	180
	percentage of revenues		7.4%
	Pro forma	39,369	40,751
	percentage of revenues	9.1%	8.0%
Diluted earnings per share	As reported	$ 2.10	$ 1.99
	Pro forma	2.10	2.00

DIGITAL WIDGETS, INC. PRACTICE

Now it's time to have some fun. Give your best thought to answering the questions below. See how accurate and comprehensive your answers are by reviewing the Answer Key materials on the next page.

TEST YOUR CORPORATE STRATEGY EXECUTION KNOWLEDGE

1. Was the CEO properly leveraged at the Blue Moon meeting?
2. What went wrong with Blue Moon and how could management improve their execution of corporate strategy at the customer interface?
3. What Pivotal Agreement opportunity was missed on the Blue Moon deal?
4. What went wrong on the OmniCor account?
5. How could the the 3D Model, including Dialogue Principles and Sales Execution Plans, be applied to the OmniCor situation to improve margins?

TEST YOUR BUSINESS ACUMEN SKILLS

After you have studied and analyzed Digital's complete set of financial statements, give some thought to answering the following questions.

1. Income statement: What is the general state of the income picture?
2. Balance sheets: What financial trends can you identify?
3. Cash flows: How is Digital Widgets, Inc., handling its cash? What conclusions can you draw from its activities?
4. Merger notes: What percentage of revenue gain comes from the mergers?
5. General assessment: What is your general assessment of the financial state of the company?
6. Red flags: What represents Digital's greatest vulnerability?

ANSWER KEY

Corporate Strategy Execution Knowledge

Here's how Digital Widgets, Inc. EVP of Sales Joe Moreno summed up the situation in his memo to CEO Robert Brentwood.

Memo

To: Robert Brentwood, CEO of Digital Widgets, Inc.
From: Joe Moreno, EVP Sales
Subject: Postmortem on Recent Execution of Corporate Strategy

As you requested, I have investigated what happened with Blue Moon in an effort to learn why we did not win the account.

Based on my extensive analysis, I have concluded there were a number of factors that contributed to our losing this valuable piece of business.

To summarize:

- We got caught up in the pricing conversations too quickly and shared information about possible discounts before establishing the value of our solution.

- We didn't fully uncover the buyer's real needs.

- While your presence always adds value, in this case, given the result, we clearly didn't leverage you the right way. In fact, I wonder if we weren't sending the message that we would do anything to make the deal.

- In retrospect, we were not calling high enough in the organization. We should have pushed back harder at the point where we asked to interview Blue Moon's executives at an earlier stage in our sales process and gotten to the CEO at that point. As you and I have discussed, if we do this early in our sales process, at some pivotal point, we always seem to get a better deal. When we don't, our deals often go south.

By the way, Blue Moon may have been gaming us, but whether or not that was the case, we needed to do a better job earlier in the sales process to make sure we ended up with the right result.

While I was looking into the answers to your questions about Blue Moon, I took the opportunity to look into another deal that we did close but at below target margins, the OmniCor deal. In this case, we did some things right and we did some things wrong.

I will start with the things we did right:

- We used the pricing software to construct our bid.

- Our sales reps were fully trained on our new seven-step sales process, which may have helped us close the business, but I'm not sure it helped us on the margin front.

- We gave OmniCor what they wanted and expanded our business, and in the process we kept it out of the hands of Lowlands Widget, who always underprices us (they've beaten us on price on the last six deals).

In spite of all this, we made a number of mistakes. When the sales process began, the buyer took immediate control by sending out an RFP, and we weren't given an opportunity to collect the information we needed to make the case for our value. As we discussed, a critical element of our success in situations like this is influencing specifications in the RFP; we need to sell in a way that avoids the RFP altogether. Clearly in this case we were not able to do that. Because of this we found ourselves making concessions that lowered the profitability of the final deal.

- Prompt payment discounts: They made the case that they've gotten them in the past, and should continue to get them. After we made this concession, I discovered

that they are out of compliance with the previous contract. If the sales rep had known, we might not have
made this concession.

- Volume buying incentives: Even though they have not
complied in the past, we are hoping to keep them honest
this time.

- Payment terms: thirty vs. sixty days. Though a concession, this won't cost more. The reality is that they are
already paying over sixty days.

- Shipping: To make the bid, we were required to provide
expedited shipping on certain large shipments without
charging extra fees.

Because our CRM doesn't provide data on account margins
yet, this information was not available to the sales team, and
they were responding to demands without all the facts at hand.
We are working with IT to move this up on their priority list. I
look forward to a full debrief on Blue Moon and OmniCor with
the entire management team tomorrow.

Robert, the fact of the matter is, we've got to execute better.

BUSINESS ACUMEN

If you studied the financial statement, ran a few ratios, and answered the
questions, you probably detected the following trends.

On the Income Statements

- The main issue is declining revenue (poor sales).

- Gross margins increased from 39 percent to 41 percent.

- SG&A expense is increasing (gross margin is increasing).

- Income before taxes has been fairly constant (however, the percentage of net income per sales capital is increasing).

- The real issue is poor sales growth.

- Digital Widgets is making acquisitions to boost revenue as an offset
to poor generic sales.

From the Balance Sheets

- Digital Widgets has been paying down debt (long-term debt went
from $41 million to $29 million—they are generating cash).

- They have been buying back stock.

- Treasury stock (under Stockholders' Equity section): Equity has
not gone up by earnings; it has gone up by buying back stock. Stock
buy-back is an effort to do something with their cash:

  - They believe buying back their stock is a good use of their
cash; prospects are good and they feel their stock price will
reflect that.
  - They are taking their money and giving money back to the
shareholders.

On the Statements of Cash Flows

- Begin with the recent year's cash flow—$56 million in cash from
operations in 2002; $77 million in 2003; $62 million in 2004. CAP

X is insignificant so it is free cash flow. They have taken this cash and bought companies, repaid $191 million in debt, and received $18 million from exercise of options.

- Digital Widgets had a gain from mergers.

From the Merger Notes

- The note shows percentage revenue gain from mergers.

General Conclusions on Creating Economic Value

- The company is well-managed from a financial perspective. The company is feeling very good about its own future. This shows in their activities: making acquisitions, buying back stock.

- The company is strong—margins have increased.

- Cash flow has been very robust ($1 of income produces $1.6 in free cash flow; very efficient).

Red Flag Issue

Sales are dropping! Digital Widgets needs to figure out how to get generic sales up through better sales execution at the customer interface.

NOTES

CHAPTER 1

1. Robert Kaplan and David Norton, *The Balanced Scorecard: Translating Strategy into Action* (Cambridge, MA: Harvard Business School Press, 1996).

2. Bain, review of *Beyond the Core: Expand Your Market Without Abandoning Your Roots*, by Chris Zook, Bain & Company. www.bain.com/bainweb/publications/wbb_books.asp (accessed November 13, 2006).

CHAPTER 2

1. Peter S. DeLisi, "Strategy Execution: An Oxymoron or a Powerful Formula for Corporate Success?" *Strategy & Leadership*, May/June 1999: 2.

2. Ibid., 3.

3. McKinsey & Company, "Building a Nimble Organization: A McKinsey Global Survey," *McKinsey Quarterly*, no. 3 (2006).

CHAPTER 4

1. Michael Marn, "The Power of Pricing," *McKinsey Quarterly*, no. 1 (2003): 1.

2. Ibid., 1.

3. Paul F. Kocourek, Walter J. Mancini, and Matthew Calderone, "The Art of Best Practice Transfer," *strategy+business*, Fourth Quarter 2002: 2.

CHAPTER 6

1. McKinsey & Company, "Building a Nimble Organization: A McKinsey Global Survey," *McKinsey Quarterly*, no. 3 (2006).
2. Malcolm Gladwell, *Blink* (New York: Little Brown, 2005) 114.
3. Ibid.

CHAPTER 9

1. M. Scott Peck, *The Road Less Traveled* (New York: Simon & Schuster, 1978).

COURSE B

1. John P. Kotter, *Leading Change* (Cambridge, MA: Harvard Business School Press, 1996) 14.

INDEX